NEW STRATEGIES FOR

REPUTATION MANAGEMENT

Gaining control of issues, crises and corporate social responsibility

ANDREW GRIFFIN

CIPR

PAGE

London and Philadelphia

Publisher's note

Every possible effort has been made to ensure that the information contained in this book is accurate at the time of going to press, and the publishers and author cannot accept responsibility for any errors or omissions, however caused. No responsibility for loss or damage occasioned to any person acting, or refraining from action, as a result of the material in this publication can be accepted by the editor, the publisher or the author.

First published in Great Britain and the United States in 2008 by Kogan Page Limited.
Reprinted in 2008
First published in paperback in 2009

120 Pentonville Road
London N1 9JN
United Kingdom
www.koganpage.com

525 South 4th Street, #241
Philadelphia PA 19147
USA

© Andrew Griffin, 2008

ISBN 978 0 7494 5633 7

British Library Cataloguing-in-Publication Data

A CIP record for this book is available from the British Library.

Library of Congress Cataloging-in-Publication Data

Griffin, Andrew, 1972-
    New strategies for reputation management : gaining control of issues, crises & corporate social responsibility / Andrew Griffin.
        p. cm.
    Includes bibliographical references and index.
    ISBN 978-0-7494-5633-7 (pbk.)
    1. Corporate image–Management. 2. Corporations–Public relations. 3. Social responsibility of business. I. Title.
    HD59.2.G75 2009
    659.2–dc22

                                                        2009017652

Typeset by JS Typesetting Ltd, Porthcawl, Mid Glamorgan
Printed and bound in India by Replika Press Pvt. Ltd.

For Roberto, Mum and Dad

Contents

Acknowledgements

I would like to thank my colleague Jonathan Howie for his excellent research work. Thanks also to colleagues Nat Davies, Mark Hamilton and Marianna Panizza for research in the early stages. I am also grateful to my fellow Regester Larkin directors Tim Johnson and Eddie Bensilum for their helpful comments on the first draft.

Finally, thanks to Mike Regester for all his advice and support on this project and for creating the environment in which it was possible.

Introduction

The workshop participants started to arrive at about 8.30 am. Half of them had their luggage with them, ready to head straight back to the airport after the day's proceedings. As we waited for everyone to arrive, the talk over coffee was of jetlag, hotel facilities and return flight times. The accents were many and varied; the job titles on the collection of business cards I was amassing were impressive. Clearly, this was a workshop that the company was taking seriously.

And so it should. This was a 'reputation management strategy workshop' and the company was a well-known global manufacturing company with a host of household brands to its name but a reputation that could be described, at best, as 'mixed'. I had been asked to facilitate the workshop, and was told that the desired output was a draft reputation strategy and plan for the next 12 months. The agenda included crisis preparedness, issues management and the social responsibility agenda.

The standard round-the-table introductions confirmed that the participants were senior representatives from operations, sales, human resources (HR), finance and legal services. And because the workshop was about 'reputation', the communications people had come mob-handed. After a little opening spiel, I kicked off the conversation proper by asking the participants to rank the following overall company objectives from one to five in order of importance: financial success; a good reputation; a happy workforce; satisfied customers and local licence to operate. All of them, except one (not the lawyer, in fact) rated 'a good reputation' as number one.

What? A good reputation is more important than financial performance? More important than the company's legal licence to operate in its various markets? More important than satisfied customers? Apparently so, because they all looked fairly happy with themselves. This was, after all, a reputation workshop so 'a good reputation' was surely the right answer. Wasn't it?

We moved on, and I asked them what they saw as their top reputation objectives for the months ahead and, after a little discussion, the group decided that the top objective was 'successful stakeholder engagement'. They obviously noticed an expression of some surprise on their facilitator's face, and felt the need to explain this further:

'We need to engage with our stakeholders', said one of the operations people, 'to understand the external climate, protect our reputation and make better business decisions.'

'And who are these stakeholders?' I asked.

'As it happens', said one of the more junior communications people round the table, 'I have our stakeholder engagement list with me on my laptop. Our PR agency has just revised it, so it's pretty up to date. Would you like to see it?'

On went the laptop and on went the projector. As the neat table started to appear faintly on the screen in front of us, we saw that five stakeholders were on the front page marked 'Priority 1': Greenpeace, Friends of the Earth, WWF, the UK Department of Trade and Industry and the US Department of Commerce.

'So, do you intend to meet these stakeholders?'

'Perhaps. Although some we will just keep up to date with key developments and send them our CSR report.'

I had seen this CSR report just a few days before the workshop. It was colourful, earnest, honest and almost entirely about the company's position on difficult issues and its response to perceived social problems. I summed up where we were so far:

'So, you are saying that your reputation is more important than any other aspect of your business, including your financial performance and employee and customer satisfaction. You are saying that your primary objective for protecting and enhancing your reputation next year is successful stakeholder engagement. At the top of the list of these stakeholders you plan to engage are three huge international environmental lobby groups and two government departments. And one of the key tools you plan to use in this engagement is your CSR report, which focuses almost exclusively on what other people say about you.'

There was a slightly uneasy silence and a bit of chair-shuffling. The workshop was clearly off to a flying start.

After a little more discussion and a 'coffee and BlackBerry break', we moved from the general to the specific. First, we discussed crisis management. The company decided that it had a good crisis management system in place, and that it had been tested fairly recently at group level in a two-hour 'desktop exercise'. However, it was agreed that there was no room for complacency and that the crisis manual should be updated and re-circulated to key staff every six months. I asked to see a copy of the crisis manual. Of the 11 senior people in attendance, only one had a copy of the company's crisis manual with him and, oddly, it was someone from finance. He produced the manual – a 70-page A4 document which, according to the date on the front page, had been printed more than a year previously. Despite this, the group claimed that there was a good 'crisis culture' in the company and that everyone knew what they had to do were a crisis to strike. After all, when the company had faced its biggest crisis – a factory explosion in 1996 in which 14 people had died – the company had managed it well and emerged with its reputation intact.

'Who in this room was involved in managing that crisis?'

No one, apparently.

'Who in this room would agree that the world has changed fairly dramatically in the last 10 years, especially in terms of media coverage of disasters and public expectations of companies?'

Everyone agreed with that.

'Who in this room would be involved in the response if a similar crisis happened today?'

About 5 out of 11 thought they would have some involvement.

'And how many of you five have been involved in a crisis exercise in the last six months?'

One of them. And, yes, it was the man from finance who had the crisis manual in his briefcase. The group decided they were perhaps less comfortable with the 'crisis culture' than they thought they were, and agreed that 'more needed to be done' to embed crisis management through the organization.

We moved on to issues management. Various issues were identified and discussed and it was generally agreed that some of the bigger ones represented the most significant threat to the company's reputation. Systems for dealing with these issues were, however, clearly much less mature than those (albeit out-of-date) procedures in place for crises.

'Normally, it would start with us', said someone from the communications department. 'If we spotted something that we thought was an issue for the company, we would escalate it and put a strategy in place for dealing with it.'

'What would that strategy look like?' I enquired.

'We would develop a position with the most appropriate internal people, and then engage with our stakeholders.'

'What does that mean?'

'Talk to them. Send them information.'

'To be honest', interjected another communications team member, 'we'd normally just have a reactive statement. We usually feel it's too risky to address the bigger issues proactively.'

'Yes', agreed one of the operations people, 'although we often feel we have a good position on an issue, we think that we'd lose the battle in the media because other stakeholders have messages with more emotional appeal. It's hard to compete with them.'

'So you think some of your stakeholders are out to get you?'

'Yes, some of them hate us whatever we do. They criticize all our reports, they jump on every issue and accuse us of acting irresponsibly. We've tried to talk to them in the past, and they seem nice enough, but there's not much in it for them to engage positively with us.'

'Which stakeholders exactly are you talking about?'

'Well, you know, the bigger NGOs.'

'Like the ones that are at the top of your stakeholder engagement list? The stakeholder engagement list that will inform your stakeholder engagement strategy next year? The stakeholder engagement strategy that is the primary objective for managing your reputation? The reputation that is more important to you than financial performance and customer satisfaction? Those stakeholders?'

More chair-shuffling. The workshop was not going quite as easily as they had expected. It was time for afternoon tea before the final 'next steps' session.

OK, so I've embellished this workshop a bit, but does any of this sound familiar? If it does, read on.

The point of recounting this workshop experience (which is, in fact, an amalgam of various discussions and workshops I have had with companies in the last few years) is to illustrate the premise of this book, which is as follows.

The world in which organizations exist and operate has changed immeasurably in the past decade or two. Demands are higher. Information-sharing is quicker. Attitudes towards global brands have changed. The spotlight on corporate performance is more intense. Whilst crises and issues remain the biggest risks to reputation, companies are now under fire even when they are not faced with a tangible immediate risk. Companies are, it seems, on a perpetual 'collision course' with the world at large.

So, companies are spending more and more money and time on 'reputation management'. Most large enlightened companies now have some sort of crisis communication manual in place, sitting alongside business continuity plans in case of serious emergency. Most also have some sort of issues management structure, ranging from rudimentary rapid media rebuttal processes to complex risk-based issue identification and management systems. Most now produce some sort of corporate responsibility report, highlighting areas the company recognizes as being of concern to stakeholders and cataloguing the company's efforts to address them. Together with local community investment, advertisement campaigns focusing on 'values' and good old-fashioned philanthropy, this all adds up to a massive endorsement, by organizations in all sectors and of all shapes and sizes, of the value of reputation.

This has all been going on for a while. It has been a good 10 years since 'reputation management' entered the corporate lexicon, and it was a catchphrase in the world of corporate communications some years before that. So, what has been the return on the reputation investment?

To be frank, not good. Although some surveys suggest that levels of trust have recovered from lows experienced immediately after the Enron and WorldCom scandals a few years ago, they are still worryingly low in most countries. Although polls vary, it generally seems that fewer than half of those surveyed say they trust companies. A study of five markets (Germany, France, the United Kingdom, the United States and Spain) by GfK NOP in early 2007 showed that over half of the 5,000 consumers surveyed felt that ethical behaviour by companies was getting worse.[1] An Institute of Business Ethics survey, also in early 2007, found that only 31 per cent of British people trust business leaders to tell the truth. This means 7 out of 10 British people think that business leaders are liars.[2] The media is still full of corporate failings, global problems and reasons to hate the powerful private sector. It seems that companies are under attack and under the reputation spotlight more now than ever before.

Something clearly isn't working.

This book looks at what isn't working, why it isn't working and what can be done about it. It argues that the mindset and language that companies use to consider reputation (as caricatured by the workshop story above) need changing. Priorities need reviewing. Strategies need revisiting. Companies need to understand that reputation is not distinct from financial performance, customer satisfaction, employee satisfaction and the like; it is the sum of all those factors and cannot be managed separately from them. Companies need to adjust to the changes in the outside world. They need to understand, and navigate more successfully, the corporate collision course. Specifically, companies need to change the way they prepare for and manage crises, improve how they deal with issues and change the terms of debate on social responsibility. Only by doing this will they start to wrest back control of their reputations.

The rest of the book is structured as follows. Chapter 1 examines in more detail how reputation is currently defined and managed by organizations. It will pick up on trends and changes as well as the significant disparities that exist in terminology, strategy and preparedness. Chapter 2 then looks at 'the corporation under fire'. From the spread of democracy to the accessibility of new technologies, various changes will be discussed to show why the external environment has become so hostile and sceptical towards business. Chapter 3 encourages organizations to change their mindsets on reputation management. It includes some key generic steps that companies can take to start the process of getting back on the reputation front foot. Chapters 4, 5 and 6 then look in turn at changes that can be made to crisis management, issues management and social responsibility. These chapters include case studies to illustrate both the mistakes of the past and the improvements that could be made for the future. Finally, Chapter 7 makes some recommendations on how organizations can turn good intentions into action and encourages them to show reputation management leadership.

This book is not an academic tome, although it does cite others' thoughts and views where relevant. It is not a compendium of case studies to show how important reputation is, although there are case studies dotted throughout the text to illustrate points. Nor is it a 'how to' guide, although there is practical advice at the end of each of the latter chapters. It is, rather, a thought piece and a 'call to change', based on my experience of advising companies on crisis management, issues management and social responsibility.

All organizations in all sectors need to concern themselves with their reputations. I hope that this book has thoughts and suggestions of interest to all, but the focus is on the private sector because it is companies that seem to be in most danger of losing their way in reputation risk management. Companies have been the primary driving force behind economic progress wherever they are able to operate freely and create wealth, but they are rewarded with suspicion. Some of this suspicion has been warranted, but much of it has not. Companies have responded to this suspicion with many genuine improvements in performance, style, social involvement and responsibility, but these are now greeted with scepticism. Companies are understandably feeling unloved, defensive and punished for their success, with their reputations seemingly in the hands of others. The time has come for them to regain the initiative in reputation management.

Notes

1. Survey findings contained in a *Financial Times* story (20 February 2007), 'Businesses Behaving Badly, Say Consumers'.
2. Institute of Business Ethics (February 2007) *Ethics Briefing: Survey on Business Ethics* (4).

1 Reputation management today

Let's start with where we are today, two decades or so into what one author has described as the 'reputation revolution'.[1] How are organizations talking about their reputations and how are they managing them?

First, everybody's talking about it. It seems that organizations of all shapes and sizes and in all sectors are fully conversant in the language of reputation. Of course, it is talked about in some countries and some companies more than others: in small organizations in developing countries, it is probably not much of a day-to-day talking point. But the evidence suggests that, for multinationals and large organizations in developed countries at least, the concept of reputation management has penetrated beyond the communications department. It is now commonplace to hear terms such as 'reputation protection', 'reputation risk management' and 'reputation strategy' at the very top of a company. Some organizations have gone so far as to include 'reputation' in the title of a senior executive: Dow has a VP of Communications and Reputation and GSK has a VP of Corporate Image and Reputation.

There are also innumerable reputation surveys and reports from PR companies, corporate ethics organizations, academics and other experts and advisers. Anyone who is a subscriber to any of these reports or journals will know the sort of findings that are uncovered. According to one such survey, 72.1 per cent of CEOs are 'very concerned' or 'somewhat concerned' about threats to their company's corporate reputation.[2]

Almost all big PR companies will now offer some sort of reputation management service. If mainstream PR companies are feeling the need to talk reputation to their clients, this is a fair indication that 'reputation' and 'reputation management' are catching on in the corporate world. This is having the unfortunate and confusing consequence of making 'building reputation', 'reputation management' and 'doing PR' interchangeable.

So, with all this reputation-speak out there, does this mean we no longer need to issue rallying cries for organizations to take reputation management seriously, to value it as their number one asset or to talk the language of reputation in the boardroom? No.

First, don't believe the polls. People, including opinion formers and CEOs, will often respond to survey questions with what they think is the 'best' answer rather than the truth. For example, 65 per cent of British people claim that they only buy energy-saving light bulbs, but only 20 per cent of the bulbs sold each year are energy-saving.[3] I am not in the least surprised by this statistic, or any of the others in *The Times* article from which it came, which is why I am sceptical when I see surveys that show that CEOs see reputation as their 'number one asset'.

Second, the question is based on the false premise that we all have a common understanding of what reputation and reputation management mean. Many organizations do take what they think is reputation management seriously, but few have really come to grips with it fully. Too many still ghettoize it in the PR department, thinking it is about social programmes or image enhancement or issues management.

Just because 'reputation' is a buzzword doesn't mean it is understood in a consistent way. And, just because 'reputation management' is something that enlightened organizations recognize they need to do doesn't mean that they are doing it. To unpick this more, we need to start with terminology.

Reputation terminology

Reputation is described by *The Penguin English Dictionary* as '1: overall quality or character as seen or judged by others; 2: fame, celebrity; 3: recognition by other people of some characteristic or ability'. This seems fairly clear.

If only it was that simple. When it comes to corporate reputation, it apparently gets more complicated. One expert has described corporate reputation as the 'perceptual representation of a company's past actions and future prospects that describes the firm's overall appeal to all of its key constituents when compared with other leading rivals'.[4] This bases reputation on the now popular 'stakeholder view of the firm', a way of looking at companies that stresses that a company's long-term licence to operate, and success, depend on its interactions with a wide network of stakeholders. Another expert writes that this 'stakeholder approach to understanding corporate reputation accommodates the new diverse and complementary approaches to measuring reputation which are designed to capture the views of all stakeholders'.[5]

Plenty of definitions exist for 'reputation management' too. Michael Morley, for example, describes this as 'the orchestration of discrete public relations initiatives designed to promote or protect the most important brand you own – your corporate reputation'.[6]

So, it seems to be something about stakeholders and public relations. And here we have the first problem. If I was an operations manager reading these definitions, or if I was a salesperson, a lawyer, a finance manager or someone who actually makes a product or sells a service in any given company, I would probably switch off right about now. Just with definitions alone, 'reputation' has already been deconstructed, overcomplicated, linked to unhelpful jargon and thereby ghettoized into the PR department. So instead, let me suggest a simpler way of thinking about reputation. Not radically different, but I hope more holistic, understandable and jargon-free.

As an individual, what people think about you matters. It affects how they treat you and whether or not they want to meet you, talk to you, listen to you, employ you and such like. The same is true of organizations. There are many people thinking different things about your organization. Some think good things; some think bad things; most won't really give it much thought at all. But, they will all be thinking their thoughts for different reasons, because they all have different ways of seeing the world. The overall impression that all these different thoughts add up to is called your 'reputation'. It's not a science, however, so it is always going to be hard for anybody to conclude whether you have a 'good' or 'bad' reputation. But, because it is better to have a good reputation than a bad one, you should know what people think about you and you should think, talk and act with this knowledge in mind. Over time, you can change this reputation by changing what you do and/or by changing how you explain what you do, although you will never get everyone thinking the same thing.

I realize that this does not fit neatly and succinctly into a 'model', a PowerPoint slide or a job description, but I make no apologies. Any attempt to deconstruct and compartmentalize corporate reputation risks missing the point: your reputation is difficult to pin down as it is based on perceptions. As the dictionary definition points out, it is judgement by others and recognition by others that create reputation. It is hard to manage because it can be affected by any part of your organization, but it must be managed because it is so important.

Reputation evaluation

So, we know it's important but we can't agree on exactly what reputation is and what reputation management entails. But do we at least know how to place a value on reputation? This is a question that has troubled reputation experts. There are various academic models that have been used in an attempt to place a value on reputation. One of the most complex is the Reputation Institute's 'RepTrak™ model' and its measurement tool, the 'RepTrak™ Pulse'. According to the company itself:

> To understand what drives the 'RepTrak™ Pulse', RI has identified 23 different attributes, grouped around seven dimensions that describe the common platform through which most organizations build reputation. In its detailed advisory work, the RI relies on sophisticated statistical analyses to connect the RepTrak™ Pulse to the underlying attributes and dimensions, and thereby identify the key drivers and action points for reputation management.

The 23 attributes include things like 'first to market' and 'adapts quickly to change' in the 'Innovation' dimension and 'supports good causes' and 'positive influence on society' in the 'Citizenship' dimension. In the United States in 2006, Kraft Foods won with a RepTrak™ Pulse of 81.82, with McDonald's languishing with a lowly Pulse of 63.82.[7]

With the greatest of respect, I find this convoluted and completely unhelpful. It is entirely understandable for experts and companies to seek ways to evaluate reputation, because it would be so powerful if we could say with any accuracy that 'your reputation is worth US$345 million a year, so you'd better manage it properly', or 'you score 67 per cent on the reputation ranking, the third lowest in your sector'. In theory, this should really sell the concept of reputation management to the sceptical. But unfortunately, reputations cannot be valued or scored like this. Reputation is not a science. Why not try standing on a street corner for an hour and asking passers-by: 'What is the value of Company X's reputation?' If you get a numerical answer, you've accidentally asked another 'behavioural' social scientist who wants to find scientific or mathematical answers to emotional questions. These models mean nothing to anybody except the people who charge a lot of money to run them for companies and they say nothing meaningful about anything.

The best way to sell reputation management is through case studies. This has been done well elsewhere[8] so I do not intend to go through a series of case studies that show that if you fail to manage your reputation, your bottom line will suffer. Suffice to say that, if you are in any doubt that losing your reputation is a bad thing to do, pop on to the internet and read up on Pan Am (post-bombing of Flight 103 in 1988), Exxon (post-*Valdez* oil spill in 1989), Nestlé (after allegations surfaced in the early 1970s about aggressive marketing of breast-milk substitutes in the developing world) or Monsanto (after it attempted to bring genetically modified food technology to the United Kingdom in 1998). You could equally look at President Clinton's approval ratings and legislative success post-Monica or Michael Jackson's music sales and financial situation after the child abuse court cases. You can argue the toss about the extent to which some of the above did anything terribly 'wrong' (Pan Am was the victim of a terror attack and Michael Jackson was acquitted) but the point is that reputations suffered regardless.

Internally, a good way to talk about the value of reputation and reputation management is to find examples in your organization of where a failure to manage reputation has cost money. For example, I worked once with a chemical company that had just spent over US$20 million cleaning up one of its sites after concerns about 'cancer-causing chemicals' had taken hold in the local community. Regulators, politicians and experts had entered the fray and the company was obliged to clean up the land to an extremely exacting standard, even though there had never been any risk to the health of anyone or anything in the first place. Using this very real and recent case study, my client and I talked to other site managers in the same company, asking them what they would be prepared to pay in terms of 'reputation insurance' against this sort of outcome. Most said they would be happy to pay between 2 per cent and 5 per cent. Even at the bottom end of that range, there is a lot of proactive reputation management work that can be done for US$400,000.

There are ways in which you can track your reputation over time. You can look at what your peers say about you in, for example, *Fortune Magazine*'s 'Most Admired Companies' index. In 2007, the top three companies in this index were General Electric, Starbucks and Toyota.[9] There are other polling data you can use. Plenty of polling organizations will gladly conduct a survey of your key markets, your key stakeholders or your key political audiences. But you might be wary of 'opinion former' polls, because opinion formers tend to form opinions for each other, but not necessarily for employees, customers and the local communities where you operate.

One often overlooked measurement is, if you are a profit-making company, your sales. If we experts are saying that a poor reputation hits the bottom line, it stands to reason that the biggest companies in the world must have the best reputations. ExxonMobil is the biggest company in the world.[10] Its revenues, according to *Fortune Magazine*'s 'Global 500' in 2006, were nearly US$340 billion.[11] It is often derided as having one of the worst corporate reputations in the world. But not, it would seem, in the eyes of its customers.

In a similar vein, a June 2006 feature article in the UK daily newspaper *The Independent* boldly stated in its subtitle that 'big brands are despised as enemies of the environment' and launched into the familiar diatribe against some of the world's biggest brands. For example: 'Coca-Cola is a symbol of American commercial imperialism and has an allegedly poor record on human rights and the environment.' In response, the company 'sponsors worldwide sports events, particularly football tournaments like the World Cup' whilst 'millions of Britons are glugging concoctions of sugary water, additives and caffeine'.[12] The other 'despised' brands in the ethics audit are Tesco, McDonald's, Gap, BP, Nestlé, Starbucks and Nike. Unless I am mistaken, these are all massively successful companies with huge consumer bases.

This is not to say that big successful companies can ignore their reputations in the knowledge that they are doing well. It means that all companies need to look at reputations more holistically, considering customer choice as well as 'key audience' opinion in the reputation mix.

Strate
m

Ryanair – the airline we love to hate?

Another example of reputation not necessarily being linked to corporate success is Ryanair, the Irish budget airline, which was voted 'the world's least favourite airline' by users of the website TripAdvisor.[13] The company's response to being told that its unfriendly staff, delays and poor legroom had helped it win this unwanted title was to say: 'The 42 million passengers who will fly with Ryanair this year have listened to real trip advice and choose Ryanair for the lowest fares and the best punctuality.'

As the business editor of *The Times* wrote when Ryanair announced huge profits in February 2007, 'O'Leary [the airline's founder] has proved that passengers on short-haul journeys do not mind putting up with a few discomforts – hard seats that don't adjust, no seatback pockets, no free towelettes – in return for lower prices. Passengers are voting with their seats.'[14] The article points out that customers are increasingly attuned to how the airline trade works, and are now used to making informed choices between budget airlines primarily on cost.

There are, of course, huge dangers in being complacent about customer concerns, and Ryanair might consider itself in a precarious position if competitors are offering the same reliable cheap service with a better 'reputation'. And, if the company were to face a genuine crisis – a crash, for example – the allegations of 'skimping on safety' might be hard to refute, even if they are untrue.

But the company and its fans have a point: product quality and price are still the overriding considerations in framing customer choices. Having a reputation for no-nonsense value for money is no bad thing.

In evaluating your reputation, companies should not forget that their customers make a choice every time they buy one of their products or services and that this choice is more powerful in effect than the opinions that customers and others may voice at other times. However, do not be complacent in success. Reputations, and customer loyalty, can change very quickly. If you manage an issue or a crisis poorly, you will soon find out the value of the reputation you have just lost.

Joined-up thinking?

So, reputation is hard to define and hard to value. And, there's another problem: it is not as intrinsic to the business as senior executives like to make out. Many of the organizations that have taken reputation fully on board realize that it is much more than PR. They now speak of 'living our values', 'being a listening organization', 'joined-up thinking' or 'effecting change throughout the organization'. But, it is difficult to say these things if you separate how you manage reputation from how you manage 'the business'.

A good illustration of this is corporate reporting. Most companies that produce a social responsibility report (which, as we shall see later, could also be entitled 'in defence of our tarnished reputation') do so entirely separately from the annual accounts report. Of course, the annual report needs to be written in a standardized way and is a stand-alone document, but there is nothing to stop companies linking the documents in terms of timing and publicity. Instead, there is one document that is all about how well the organization has done financially, and another saying that it is an organization doing its best to be mindful of its responsibilities and its reputation. They sit nicely side, in matching colours. But, they are separate, none that they are published and publicized at different times. s this separation mean that reputation is more important than the business, or less important?

To know where any organization's true priorities lie, you only need to ask one thing: do you reward your management and staff based on increased profits or improved reputation? Some might answer that they have reward programmes for community initiatives and such like, but these are, of course, additional to normal remuneration (and tend to be few and far between). Some might say that the two are interlinked: 'We have improved our reputation, so our sales have shot up and so have bonuses.' Maybe. But, in a big company, management reports up the figures first and foremost.

Imagine a large manufacturing company with operations all over the world. It is the end of the financial year, and two local managers are reporting up to head office. One says: 'Our profits have fallen slightly this year, although we feel we are much more integrated into the local community, we have held various successful crisis management tests and we have managed various bits of negative media coverage with no knock-on effect to our reputation.' The other says: 'We have delivered 45 per cent more profit this year than last year, despite the fact that there are some unresolved issues with the local community and we had an incident that got some bad press.' Who's getting the bigger bonus? Who's in line for promotion?

Assuming you agree that the profit-generator gets the bigger bonus and the better career prospects, the next question is whether that is a bad thing. This, in microcosm, is the 'profits versus principles' debate that companies find so troublesome. Does the fact that companies reward primarily on financial performance mean they are just paying lip service to reputation?

Well, yes and no. Certainly it is difficult to respond to a survey saying 'Sustainability is our top priority' or 'We will put principles before profit' if your organization still rewards staff almost exclusively on profit numbers. So if we continue to consider reputation separately from other aspects of the business, then we are essentially laying ourselves open to the charge of hypocrisy. We are in danger of saying: 'Reputation is our most important asset and we invest a lot in managing our reputation. However, it's not as important as financial performance, which is how we judge success and rewards.' Companies may say that reputation is in the boardroom and that it is their 'most important asset', but if it is treated in a way that separates it from operational and financial performance, it will never be top of the board agenda.

This does not mean that we need to turn business models on their heads. To suggest that companies reward management on the basis of something as subjective as reputation would challenge the whole basis of capitalism, and it is only through capitalism that we have got to a stage in the world's economic and social development that we can afford the luxury of debating reputation.[15]

The answer, perhaps, is that companies should celebrate profit and success more publicly and more brazenly than they do, and merge it with reputation. Financial success means that customers are buying products and services, more wealth can be created and more jobs provided. That's business, and that's good. So companies could report more like this:

> We've done fantastically well this year. We've made more money than ever before and we have more employees than ever before. We think our products are great and so, apparently, do our customers. We want to make sure this keeps going so we create more wealth, so we are keen to ensure that, on balance, the people who matter to us think we're doing what we do in a responsible way. Those people are our employees, our customers and, where we have large operations, our neighbours.

That's probably what most companies think, but it's not quite what they say. There's more along these lines in Chapter 3.

To finish off this section on 'reputation theory', I would advocate getting into a new mindset about the meaning of reputation, perhaps by finding new ways to use the word. For example: 'We have a great reputation for making products that consumers love at a price they can afford', or 'We have a fantastic reputation for getting our customers from A to B on time, without fuss and at low-cost.' It's a small step in the journey to regaining the reputation initiative, but it is an important one as it recognizes that reputation is not just about ethics, sustainability and responsibility. Reputation is about everything that an organization does, how it does it and how its customers and other audiences think, feel and act as a result.

Aspects of managing reputation risk

Does all this mean reputation is indefinable and unmanageable because it is so inseparable and all-encompassing? Of course not. Organizations have to deconstruct things into manageable chunks, otherwise nothing would ever get done. But, what is important is that they should reconstruct it when talking about it and ensure it becomes part of the whole organization's culture.

As we will see below and through the rest of this book, there are three components of reputation management that can be separated and managed in different ways, but they must be considered as separated through management necessity only. They all essentially point at the same thing: understanding the importance of, and the need to look after, the organization's reputation. These three components are:

- crisis management;
- issues management;
- social responsibility.

So now we have 'deconstructed' into these three components of managing risk to reputation, how are companies doing in crisis management, issues management and social responsibility? In 2006, the company I run conducted an audit of the reputation risk management practices of various clients and other organizations. An independent consultant conducted qualitative interviews with a good cross-section of companies in various sectors. There were various interesting conclusions, four of which are explained below.

Conclusion one – terminology is extremely diverse

Not only is reputation defined and discussed in different ways by different organizations, the terms 'crisis management' and 'issues management' are not as universally accepted and understood as one might imagine. Whilst most respondents to our audit claimed that reputation management was a term that was widely used in their organization, only a few admitted to feeling uneasy about how the term was used and implemented through the organization. Of those who did have concerns, one comment from one senior communications professional (who had 'nominal ownership' of the company's reputation) summed up this concern: 'I don't like the term reputation management', she said, 'and I try to avoid it. It implies that it is in the hands of the few, whereas, of course, it is in everyone's hands.'

'Crisis' is, for some organizations, a dirty word. Some think it is unnecessarily alarmist and prevents, rather than encourages, people from taking ownership and responsibility. Some think that using the word induces a negative crisis mentality, which makes a bad situation worse. 'Incident management' seems to be a popular alternative, with 'emergency response', 'event management' and 'special situations' other variations on the theme. I can understand 'incident management' and 'emergency response' for physical incidents, but not for the many other sorts of corporate crises that can strike. 'Event management' sounds too much like organizing a cocktail party and 'special situations' just sounds sinister and military. I'm not sure that any of these alternative phrases quite communicate what is captured by 'crisis'.

For some local or product divisions within global companies, the term 'crisis' is avoided, because to use it would take the power of managing the crisis away from these divisions and give it to some distant headquarters or regional office, which, it is rightly or wrongly assumed, will hinder rather than help the process of resolution. Office politics, tribalism and jealousies are not easily overcome, even in (or especially in) a crisis.

Some companies, by contrast, are more than happy to talk the language of crisis. A popular response to the question about terminology in our audit was to say: 'We have crises every day.' This was often said in a tone that implied that the bad news comes rather too thick and fast. One respondent said that his organization 'doesn't talk about issues, just degrees of crisis'. I have a picture of them all running around the office like headless chickens, thinking everything that comes their way is a crisis that will lead to the organization's downfall. When pushed further on what genuinely constituted a crisis, he said that it was just a 'judgement call'. Another communications director simply said: 'If the Chief Executive thinks it's a crisis, it's a crisis. If he doesn't, I guess it is my job to stop it becoming one.'

Issues management is actually more accepted as a term but, depending on the company, it can cover everything from international challenges such as global warming and child labour to the everyday tricky enquiry from a local journalist. For some, issues management is just corporate relations ('I manage issues all the time'), whilst for others it entails a complex structure and process.

It seems odd that the same words can be used to describe quite different activities, depending on the organization. It certainly makes it hard to say 'Issues management and crisis management are the key disciplines in managing your reputation', when there are at least three words or phrases in that sentence that are defined very inconsistently.

I like the term 'reputation risk' because it covers both acute reputation risks (crises) and chronic reputation risks (issues). It is a bit like the difference between an emergency room and a regular ward in a hospital. You need looking after if you are in either, but you are treated differently if you are at acute risk from how you would be treated if you had a chronic illness.

It is crucial for any organization to know the difference between a crisis and an issue, because they need to be managed in different ways. The reason that companies have crisis procedures is because they recognize that crises are special and distinct events in which external scrutiny is high, reputations are on the line immediately and fast and decisive actions and communication are needed. The crisis procedures, as will be discussed later, normally demand various members of the organization's senior management to drop everything and become part of a crisis team. Issues do not have the same sense of immediate scrutiny and urgency. This does not make them any less of a threat to reputation, but it does mean that a little more space and time is available to develop responses and make changes. An issue should not be managed like a crisis and vice versa.

Conclusion two – issues management is not taken as seriously as crisis management

There is no doubt that crises (or incidents, special situations or whatever they are called) are seen as the most serious threats to reputation. For many companies, reputation management is all about preparing for and managing crises; everything else is just an occasional local difficulty. Our audit found that organizations are far more likely to be 'crisis-ready' than prepared for any other risk to reputation and that this primacy of crises amongst reputation risks has been further strengthened by the current climate of potential global terror.

This may seem logical – surely there is nothing more threatening to a corporation than a huge physical crisis? But it is a mistake to think along these lines and a mistake to treat issues management less seriously than crisis management. I would argue that the easiest reputation risks to manage are those physical crises that are done *to* a company rather than done *by* a company, especially if part of a wider attack or event: this is because the spotlight will not be on you as a company alone, expectations will be lower, blame will not be a factor at least in the short term and the incident is the easiest to prepare for in terms of evacuations, informing next of kin, expressing public empathy and so on. In contrast, those issues that are about your organization alone, which attract long-term public attention and call into question your products, services, way of operating or very existence, are much harder to manage and can result in much greater long-term reputation damage.

For example, after the London bombings of 7 July 2005, one client with Central London headquarters called me to say that they had 'managed the crisis very well' and that 'if we can manage that, surely we're ready for anything'. In November of that year, what seemed like a minor employment issue was all over the company's trade press and was still causing it significant distress and reputation damage some months later. Reputation risk is illogical and unscientific: although it seems that one risk should bring greater scrutiny and potential damage than another, it does not always work like that.

If organizations focus solely on preparing for the big events, perfecting the crisis manual and testing their crisis systems, they might miss some real reputation-damaging issues creeping up out of nowhere. Professor Ian Mitroff, a US-based crisis academic, puts this well. He says that CM (crisis management) is in danger of a 'hostile takeover' by RM (risk management) and business continuity planning (BCP): 'RM and BCP threaten to reduce CM to a series of structured exercises and checklists. The compulsive need for structure and certainty has led far too many organizations to buy into the techniques of RM and BCP.' His argument is that crisis management (and, I think, reputation management in general) is far more emotional than the more procedures-driven risk management and business continuity planning.[16]

So, whilst crisis management may be more intense, higher-profile and easier organizationally to box and manage, it doesn't necessarily mean it is more important than issues management. Some organizations have realized this, but most have not.

Conclusion three – asset-rich companies lead the way in the field

This is not surprising, but the difference in crisis preparedness is marked. In fact, there are three basic categories of company in terms of preparedness: companies with major tangible assets (primarily in the extractive and transport industries, together with travel companies); physical product-led companies (pharmaceuticals, food and consumer goods) and service industries. The asset-rich companies typically have strong disaster management capabilities and some sort of issues management structure. The physical product-led companies are often well-versed in the art of product recalls. The service industry is the least prepared of all for a major crisis or issue.

If you think about it, this seems to make sense. Companies with big assets (refineries, factories, infrastructure) should be prepared for crises affecting these assets. Companies with consumer-facing products should be prepared to deal with crises affecting these products (faults in cars, contaminated food, exploding electrical goods). And, service industry companies are all about people, expertise and time rather than products.

But if you think about it more, it makes no sense at all. First and foremost, the world has changed and the sorts of crises and issues that companies face today are not just the crashes, bangs, spills and product faults that companies started to learn to deal with in the public eye some decades ago. Second, companies with assets and popular physical products have something tangible to their name, whereas the service industry has nothing but its reputation. If the quality and integrity of their people and their service is called into question, reputation can be lost with nothing to fall back on.

Accountants Arthur Andersen found this out after its alleged role in the Enron collapse. Despite the fact that the company won an appeal against its conviction for obstructing justice in the Enron case, the name once associated with excellence and integrity became associated with scandal and deceit. Its employees and clients deserted the company, which then ceased trading in 2004. Arthur Andersen had built and maintained an excellent reputation over nearly 100 years, but this reputation disappeared in a matter of weeks, and the company spiralled to an ignominious end shortly thereafter.

From Google to Goldman Sachs, Lazard to lastminute.com, companies in the service sector trade on their name and their brand. So, shouldn't they be as prepared to face reputation risks as asset-rich companies? The reason they are not is an accident of historical definitions. Crisis management today is based on disaster recovery techniques pioneered by asset-rich companies some decades ago. This approach is now out of date.

But there is no need for complacency amongst the asset-rich and physical-product-driven companies. They may have a head start on the service industry in terms of reputation management, but the race is going in a different direction. All companies in all sectors need to be able to cope with the new breed of reputation risks of the 21st century.

Conclusion four – social responsibility is poorly defined and managed 'elsewhere'

The fourth conclusion of our audit was that 'corporate social responsibility' is understood and implemented very inconsistently and that few respondents felt that they wanted to take ownership of it. A popular response was a roll of the eyes and an 'Oh, that'. Separate from the audit, I recently had a meeting with one client who had just moved jobs from one multinational to another. He told me that he'd moved from one company that 'has a really good internal understanding of CSR, but never does anything as it hasn't really got a home' to another that 'is doing so many things that constitute CSR but doesn't have anyone pulling it all together, which means the outside world assumes we're doing nothing'.

Of those who responded to our audit, plus others with whom my colleagues and I have discussed CSR in recent months, the majority believe that CSR is important but that it is too 'all-encompassing' or 'unwieldy' or 'ill thought-through' in their organization. The fact that it has been jumped all over by big PR companies that try to convince their clients that CSR is the 'must-have' service of the moment does not help and does not go down well. As one contact recently said: 'PR people have tried to turn CSR into the things that they know they can do, which is why it is all about glossy reports, lofty commitments and sponsoring the local softball team.' There's certainly some truth in that.

Currently, it seems that if you were to ask companies for an example of something they were doing in the field of CSR, you would get a response that included one or more of the following elements:

● brand-led cause-related marketing initiatives, which openly position a brand alongside a good cause or charity;

- independent corporate social investment, not linked to a particular brand and often involving the giving of time and expertise as well as money;
- reporting on compliance, whether to external or internal standards of business;
- reporting on issues, such as how the organization is responding to concerns it has received or major issues of the day;
- donations.

Different countries emphasize different elements of the above list. In the United States, social responsibility has traditionally been associated with charitable giving, whilst in France the term is more closely linked with employee relations. In the United Kingdom, there is a more ethical dimension to social responsibility.

There is nothing intrinsically wrong with any of the above, but there is something not quite right about the overall term and the way in which companies 'do' CSR today. It is partly in the phrase itself: 'corporate social responsibility programmes' inherently suggest that they correct corporate social irresponsibility, just as 'ethical business' is a response to claims that business is unethical. No wonder it is interpreted in so many ways by different companies and no wonder, as we found in our audit, it is not something that corporate communications people want to embrace and own. There is much more on CSR in Chapter 6.

Reputation management: some company caricatures

The findings of our audit were interesting, but in many ways unsurprising. They helped reinforce in my mind some of the caricatures of the sorts of organizations I come across in the field of reputation management. I thought I would conclude this section on where reputation management is today with a sketch of some of these caricatures. These are 'grotesques', but you may be able to spot some familiar people and traits from your organization.

Crisis obsessed, but otherwise unprepared

Organizations displaying these characteristics are often medium-sized companies in traditional asset-rich industries such as energy, transport and manufacturing. The need for physical crisis preparedness has been understood and implemented for decades but, like the boardroom decor, not much has moved on since the 1970s.

The crisis manual was written by, and remains in the hands of, portly men in pinstripes who work for 'risk' or 'security'. They know exactly how long it takes to get a fire crew from the local depot to each of their sites, but they have never met a single soul in the communities around these sites. Fires, kidnaps and other calamities will probably be well-handled from an operational viewpoint, but the communications people will only be allowed to join the crisis team after the decisions have been made. The new risks to reputation are not even on the radar screen and 'social responsibility' consists almost entirely of sponsoring exhibitions and donating to the Chairman's favourite charity.

Reputation by systems

These companies are often the big beasts of the corporate world who have been through a reputational bad spell some years previously, and have invested a huge amount of time and money in systems to prevent it ever happening again. Complex processes have been introduced that, when implemented well, will ensure reputation is safeguarded from any possible risk.

At least, that's the theory. Unfortunately, the systems are often over-engineered to the extent that they are impenetrable. If, God forbid, something terrible crops up that presents a serious reputation risk, everyone spends so much time consulting their systems and toolkits for dos and don'ts, hints and tips, guidance, checklists and protocols that, by the time they have decided who is in charge and what action should be taken, the issue has moved on. In these organizations, people spend more time managing the system than managing the risk, and the system becomes a straitjacket to, rather than an enabler of, good reputation risk management.

Great culture, bad structure

These organizations are the archetypal 'great place to work', with 'co-workers' feeling empowered and appreciated. The value of reputation is genuinely felt at the heart of the company, and everyone feels the pain when something goes wrong. Some issues are managed sensitively and effectively, but others are not quite addressed in as comprehensive a way as required. A sense of denial can creep in, and some might discretely distance themselves from the problem, which must have been created by someone else. And, when something really goes wrong, the hierarchy and discipline to put it right is missing. This is typically found in fairly young companies where every day is a dress-down day, and where the assets are only the people and the brand.

Overconfident

'It will never happen to us and, even if it did, we have got bright people at the top who will sort the mess out.' This attitude is found amongst those smaller companies, set up by entrepreneurs, which don't seem to last long. No systems. No training. No idea. Enough said.

Reputation evangelists

Often found in wealthy but controversial industries, these companies have bought wholeheartedly into all aspects of reputation management, so much so that they risk losing the instinct that made them so successful in the first place. The company is packed with communications people who used to work for charities and environmental or human rights lobby groups and who want to work for a company that ends war and cures hunger. The senior management regularly 'engages' with the long list of stakeholders and apologizes for anything that any audience believes is bad. This just encourages more people to criticize the company and get something out of it, creating a vicious circle of reputation initiatives and reputation damage.

There are intelligent, worthy and earnest people in head office, but there is a massive disconnect between them and the people at the coalface. The situation just doesn't add up, and the evangelists end up with two audiences – themselves and their counterparts in other industries. They slap each other on the back at reputation and ethical business conferences whilst their colleagues in operations and sales get on with the job of making and selling the products and services.

Summary

There is a lot of good work going on in crisis management, issues management and social responsibility, and I have not properly captured the 'good news' in this chapter. This is partly because I think this has been done elsewhere, and partly because I do not see a case for any company to be self-congratulatory. In reputation management today, I would characterize the corporate approach as defensive, compartmentalized and piecemeal.

Why is this?

Companies are still basing their strategies on the external world as it was about 20 years ago: a world in which the biggest reputation risk was a massive physical disaster, a world in which the only stakeholders were political decision-makers who could be persuaded and lobbied, a world in which trouble in a distant operation took days if not longer (or if at all) to reach the media in the countries that mattered. They are doing this partly because the need for structure and manageable 'boxes' has led organizations to concentrate on what former US Defence Secretary Donald Rumsfeld might describe as the 'known unknowns' of crashes and bangs and spills. This has meant that those companies who do not face that sort of risk are some way behind others who do. But the reputation risk world of today is all about a plethora of 'unknown unknowns' – the collision course of modern business. In short, organizations are prepared for the world of 1990, not the world of 2010. It is this dangerous new world that is explored in Chapter 2.

Notes

1. Genasi, C (2002) *Winning Reputations: How To be Your Own Spin Doctor*, Palgrave Macmillan, Basingstoke, p xi.

2. *PRWeek* (2004) *CEO Survey 2004.*

3. *The Times* (8 November 2006) 'The Green Divide'.

4. Fombrun, C (1996) *Reputation: Realizing Value from the Corporate Image*, Harvard Business School Press, Boston, MA, p 72.

5. Larkin, J (2003) *Strategic Reputation Risk Management*, Palgrave Macmillan, Basingstoke, p 43.

6. Morley, M (2002) *How to Manage Your Global Reputation*, Palgrave Macmillan, Basingstoke, p 10.

7. The US results of the Global RepTrak™ Pulse Project 2006 can be found at: http://www.forbes.com/2006/11/20/leadership-companies-reputation-lead-managing-cx_hc_1120usrep_slide_2.html?boxes=custom. Accessed on: 13 June 2007.

8. See Regester, M and Larkin, J (2005) *Risk Issues and Crisis Management*, Kogan Page, London.

9. *Fortune Magazine* (2007) 'America's Most Admired Companies'.

10. *Fortune Magazine* (2006) 'Global 500'.

11. Ibid.

12. *The Independent* (8 June 2006) 'The Ethics Audit 2006'.

13. *The Guardian* (26 October 2006) 'Ryanair – The World's Least Favourite Airline'.

14. *The Times* (6 February 2007) 'O'Leary Shows Us That Less is More in Air Travel'.

15. As Steve Hilton and Giles Gibbons say in the introduction to their excellent book *Good Business*: 'Reliable collective social welfare provision on a mass scale is impossible without capitalism. New technologies and strategies to protect the environment are impossible without capitalism. Improving the quality of life for the poorest people on our planet is impossible without capitalism. And capitalism is impossible without profit-making companies, or to use the faintly more sinister-sounding term employed by their critics, corporations.' See Hilton, S and Gibbons, G (2002) *Good Business*, Texere, London, p 3.

16. Mitroff, I (2005) *Why Some Companies Emerge Stronger and Better from a Crisis*, Amacom, New York, p xv.

2 The corporation under fire

The world in which corporate reputations are managed is very different now from the one of 20 years ago. This is pretty much an unchallengeable statement, as we all know that the media have become more intrusive and demanding, NGOs have become ubiquitous and individuals throughout the world have become more empowered through the extension of democracy and the growth of information technology.

For any organization, the consequence of these changes is that its reputation is even harder to manage. Especially if you are one of the bigger and more successful companies, there are many interested parties battling for a share of voice about, and influence over, your reputation.

Look, for example, at the financial services industry. The financial services industry has never been regarded as being in the forefront of reputation risk management. Risk is hardly a new concept to financial services companies – financial risk management has been around a fair while longer than reputation risk management – but as a service-based industry, it has neither the physical assets nor products that would put it at the natural forefront of reputation risk management. But this industry has in recent years seen both its profile and its reputation risks increase dramatically.

Twenty years ago, what would cause a large financial services company to be under intense external scrutiny and to be in the reputation spotlight? Perhaps the most significant risk would have been large-scale financial scandal, such as that experienced by Barings bank thanks to its 'rogue trader', Nick Leeson. Other risks would have included the financial failure of a policy or product, perhaps, and mergers and acquisitions. There were also issues to do with overseas investment – the legacy of the consumer boycott over the banking sector's presence in apartheid South Africa still haunts some financial institutions.

Today, these reputation risks remain, but have been joined by many others. The threat of terrorism against financial targets and the threat of pandemic diseases hitting service sector industries (as well as other industries) have persuaded financial services companies to up their game on crisis management. In 2006, London hosted what was one of the world's biggest ever business continuity exercises when various businesses and government agencies participated in a bird flu outbreak scenario.

But the need for crisis preparedness on this scale in the sector is just the beginning. I recently saw the contents list of a financial services company's AGM briefing pack for its Chairman. It was a catalogue of reputation risks that contained over 100 issue briefs from matters such as 'financial exclusion', 'security (identity theft)' and 'consumer finance (ethical)' to 'oppressive regimes', 'ethical reporting' and 'cleaners (living wage)'.

The latter was presumably added to the list after the demonstration held by Goldman Sachs contract cleaners shortly after the company's record bonuses were announced in November 2006. In late November and December 2006, cleaners who worked for some of London's major financial firms undertook a short but visible campaign that aimed to put an end to their 'poverty wages'. Members of the Transport and General Workers Union (T&G) organized a demonstration at the offices of Goldman Sachs. This received some media interest, as it coincided nicely with the bank's announcement of results (profits of US$16.46 billion) and high bonuses. The President of the T&G commented that 'The city fat cats are living the high life whilst cleaners are scraping by on poverty wages. It is obscene and unjust, and makes a mockery of the claims by big business that they exercise any corporate social responsibility.'[1]

This contents list is an extraordinary reflection of the modern world of reputation risk: over 100 issues that are so potentially damaging to the reputation of a company that they are thought worthy of a special brief for the Chairman ahead of the AGM.

Also, it is a sector that is targeted on issues that it might well think it doesn't really own. The funding of controversial projects in the developing world is the best example of this. Using a tactic borrowed from the animal rights movement, NGOs are increasingly targeting the "moneymen" behind new dams, mines, refineries and other infrastructure developments if they feel that there is an environmental concern or that a local community is being trampled over. If the lender's brand is better known than that of the borrower, there is even greater likelihood that the finance providers will be brought into the issue.

Finally, the sector faces more than a long list of potentially tricky issues and calamitous crises, which may or may not pop up once in a while. In many developed countries, it faces – permanently – an external social and political environment that is at best sceptical and suspicious, and, at worst, hostile.

But we should not feel sorry for financial services companies, or indeed any companies. They have brought this upon themselves. The international triumph of capitalism over other economic models has created more democracies and more consumers using more sophisticated technologies to organize, demand and expect more from companies. This is absolutely as it should be – expansion of demand is part of the corporate philosophy and has created global markets from which companies benefit enormously. But are companies as ready as they should be to manage their reputations in a world in which more and more people enjoy the benefits of global capitalism and then use them to bring permanent pressure to bear on these companies for issues that used to be in the domain of government? Do companies even fully understand their role in the new world order?

These are the questions that this chapter seeks to address. To do this, it will focus on the following six points that characterize the predominant external context in which reputations are managed today:

- The world is freer and smaller.
- It is a world of fear.

- It is a world of information.
- Individuals are empowered.
- NGOs are empowered.
- Governments remain powerful, whilst corporate power is waning.

The world is freer and smaller

I know it's a truism, but the world *is* getting smaller. The main reasons for this are, fairly obviously, the developments in information technology and the accessibility and affordability of international travel. We take much of this for granted in the developed world nowadays, but it was less than two decades ago when international telephone calls were prohibitively expensive, the internet was unheard of, there were only a handful of television channels to watch and holidays were generally taken not too far from home.

Our horizons are broader. Events – from wars to natural disasters – that used to feel distant and foreign now seem much closer to home. Whereas US military casualties in the Iraq war are extremely low compared with those suffered during World War II and Vietnam (approximately 3,000 compared with 400,000 and 60,000 respectively), every US death in the Iraq war is a media story and every grieving family member is a potential media interviewee. And, whereas it took the BBC weeks to get footage from the Armenian earthquake of 1988, it took just minutes before pictures of the Iranian earthquake of 2003 and the Asian tsunami of 2004 reached our screens. Similarly, we are far more aware of how the world economy is interlinked and interdependent. We never used to think about where our toys and clothes were made; now we have seen pictures of them being made in Asian factories.

For companies, this means that there really is no such thing as a 'little local difficulty' in some distant outpost that will never make it to the news agenda. Something that happens today at an operation in Indonesia is not only potentially front page news in the *Washington Post* tomorrow, it is also potentially the top story on CNN and the headline of a blogger's latest offering today.

Not only is there nowhere to hide in this small world, there is also no time to even think about hiding. Time, that most wonderful of luxuries when reputations are under threat, is in increasingly short supply. The days of: 'Something's happened; let's meet tomorrow first thing to discuss it' are gone. It is now far more likely to be: 'Something's happened – I just saw it on CNN and half the world's journalists seem to be outside the building.'

As an example, in 1999, the holiday company Thomas Cook had a major crisis to manage when a coach crash in South Africa killed 27 of its holidaymakers and a local tour guide. The company responded to the crisis almost impeccably, getting family members, trauma counsellors and crash specialists out to South Africa immediately and issuing press statement after press statement to feed the hungry media. But the then Managing Director, Simon Laxton, has since told of how he was informed of the crash and, within minutes, was watching helicopter footage of the crash site in South Africa live on television in his office in Peterborough, England. He knew he had to mobilize his staff and invoke his crisis procedures immediately to have any chance of managing the crisis from the front. For visual crises in particular, there is often almost no thinking time before a public response is required.

This small world is also a free world. Over the past 50 years, the proportion of countries that are democracies has risen from 14 per cent to over 60 per cent, and the proportion of people living in a democracy has risen from 31 per cent to 58 per cent.[2] In many countries, where questioning authority and demanding change were once extremely rare, individuals, communities and consumers are becoming more aware of their rights, their powers and their abilities to effect change in both the public and private sectors.

Even in countries that are not democracies, expectations over access to information and demands on authorities are increasing. The chemical spill in China in late 2005 showed that almost no regime is now immune to media attention and 'people power'.

On 13 November 2005, there was an explosion at a petrochemical plant in Jilin city. Eight days later, water to Harbin city (downstream from Jilin) was cut off and the local government cited mains maintenance as the cause. The Harbin government initially denied reports that the cause of its water shutdown was industrial poisoning, saying it was just a rumour. But two days later, after media questioning, the authorities admitted that high levels of benzene caused the water supply stoppage. A key contributing factor to the government's turnaround was the appearance of angry citizens on Chinese internet sites. The spill resulted in the resignation of Xie

Zhenhua, China's Minister of State for Environmental Protection Administration.

The hitherto docile Chinese media took a far more aggressive line, asking why disclosure of a health risk to local communities had taken so long. Beijing's *Zhongguo Qingnian Bao* (*China Youth Daily*) described the government's decision to cover up the accident as an 'unjustifiable lie', saying: 'Although the truth was revealed this time, the aftermath of the previous "lies" persists and has reduced public trust in the government.' Shanghai's *Dongfang Zaobao* (*Eastern Morning News*) wrote that: 'The panic and chain reaction caused by the failure to make information public will do great harm to the government's credibility.'[3]

China is still a long way from the sort of outrage and recriminations that would result from a similar industrial accident in Western democracies, but this incident showed that the march of (genuine) people and consumer power, backed up by global media and information sources, is ultimately unstoppable.[4]

I recently did some work in the Philippines, helping with the communication of an excellent (but in some quarters controversial) environmental improvement project. There is much poverty in metropolitan Manila, but even in the poorest areas, some local community members were not only organized but were communicating electronically with local, national and international stakeholders. It presented new challenges for the companies involved in the project, but was an entirely welcome difference from the years of unquestioned authority in that country just a few short decades ago.

Where companies have lost obliging and unorganized communities separated by distance and language, they have gained intelligent and opinionated customers united by communication and information technology. This is a trade-off that should be welcomed but which requires a strategic global approach to reputation risk management.

It is a world of fear

One of the slides I use in risk management training sessions consists simply of two photographs – a black and white one of workers sitting what seems like hundreds of feet up on the girders of a half-built skyscraper, eating sandwiches on their lunch break; and a more recent one of an office environment in South Korea in which all employees are wearing anti-SARs face masks. The question at the bottom of the slide is: 'How did we get from there to here?'[5]

Fear is a fundamentally important part of the external climate that companies face today. It seems that, in developed countries at least, the fewer worries we have in our immediate lives, the more time we have to worry about theoretical or even non-existent risks. Not that long ago, most humans were far too concerned about where the next meal was coming from and whether there was shelter for the night to concern themselves about the health implications of living near an industrial site. It would have seemed ridiculous even 50 years ago for people to worry about whether chemical residues in a nearby site might increase their chances of getting cancer at some stage of their life (already about a one in three chance in some countries) by one in a million (to a one in 3.000001 chance). And yet this is the situation that we have in developed countries today.

Partly as a result of the world of information and freedom in which we now live, our attitudes towards risk have changed. Whereas once we accepted a certain amount of risk associated with our lives and jobs, we now want a zero risk environment. We still want all the trappings of a modern consumer economy, of course: the debate about mobile phone masts and handsets being potentially damaging to health is still raging in some communities, but few people seem so worried that they actually change their mobile phone usage.

The decline in the perception of science as impartial and truth-seeking is an intrinsic part of this shift in perceptions and demands. Scientists used to be seen as the people in white coats delivering progress for humankind; now they are too often seen as the people in grey suits delivering profit for the private sector. 'Chemicals' used to be associated with progress; now it is a dirty word.

This is an important part of a general decline in trust for traditional authorities. Surveys suggest that our trust in politicians, the church, scientists, business leaders, the police and just about everybody else has gone down.[6] So whom do we trust? The answer to that question when asked in surveys is increasingly: 'People like me'. We trust people who think like and have the same sort of outlook and concerns as ourselves. That's why all the oil companies have gone down the route of using 'ordinary people' in their print and broadcast advertising: suddenly, all the advertisements seem to show an ordinary person dealing with an ordinary day job, and doing their bit to make an extraordinary difference: 'My name is Peter/Paul/Mary and I work for Shell/Exxon/BP' and so on.

An interesting example of how zero tolerance to risk has triumphed over all other concerns occurred recently in a factory in England. When airborne asbestos was found during a random external check, at levels that presented a theoretical risk to employees, the factory owners applied the precautionary principle and suspended all operations. A few months later, after further exhaustive tests, it was proven that no employee had been exposed to dangerous levels of asbestos and that the initial sample may have been flawed. But this was little comfort to the factory workers, all of whom had lost their jobs. The factory's customers had simply gone elsewhere and the company had had no choice but to close the facility permanently.

In retrospect, should the company at the centre of the asbestos scare have kept the factory operational until further tests either confirmed or refuted the initial findings? No. The laws of the risk-free world demand that responsible companies must always err on the side of caution, even when the consequences in terms of livelihoods are far more real than the theoretical health risks. As the developed world seeks to impose its standards on the developing world, there will be many more cases around the globe where jobs and livelihoods are lost because of an extremely small health and safety risk.

An awareness of and healthy attitude towards risk is certainly a good thing and I am not for a minute suggesting that modern health and safety practices are a bad development. Of course, businesses need to be far more sensitive to risk, whether real or perceived. But there must surely be a balance between genuine improvements in quality of life and tolerating increasingly bizarre claims, often based on junk science and propagated by the media, which scare us into ever-more stringent regulation and demands.

Might the pendulum swing back from the 'zero risk' mentality to a sensible approach to risk? It doesn't seem likely, given other factors in the new reputation climate and the interests of the various players who are at the moment dominating the debate.

It is a world of information

It is estimated (I don't know how) that an average US or EU citizen receives between 5,000 and 10,000 pieces of information every day.[7] Our expectations on information have changed dramatically since the advent of the internet and the trend towards more public freedom of information from governments. We expect to be able to find out almost anything within a few minutes of surfing the net.

'The media' is becoming an inadequate catch-all term for the plethora of information sources available to us now. There are various ways of deconstructing 'the media' into manageable chunks, but for the purposes of this section I will refer to 'traditional media' and 'online media'.

Traditional media

Twenty years ago, watching the news on television meant watching a half-hour or hour-long slot on one of a few terrestrial channels at some stage during the evening. You can now watch the news at any time of the day on one of many 24/7 news channels, on the internet or even on a 'podcast', but there are still news slots that are recognized as being the prime news programmes of the day (in the United Kingdom, for example, it is the *Six O'Clock News* or *Ten O'Clock News* on the BBC, *Newsnight* on BBC2, *Channel 4 News* at 7.00 pm or *ITV News* at 10.30 pm). If someone asks you 'Did you see the news last night?' they are normally referring to one of these programmes. If your organization is involved in some sort of issue or crisis that is covered on one of these slots, it is a fairly serious situation.

The 24/7 news channels may be some way behind these prime-time news slots in terms of viewing figures, but their development has had an extraordinary effect on news gathering and reporting in general. By virtue of needing to fill a channel for 24 hours a day, they need more news, they need in-depth coverage of news and they need opinion and commentary from whoever will give it. And, as they are operating in a competitive news-gathering market, they need to be quick about it.

What does this mean for reputation management? First, the 24/7 news channels tend not to find completely different stories from the news programmes of mainstream channels, but they do need to fill up more time talking about them. Whereas a story about, for example, an airline strike might take up three to four minutes on the mainstream news channel, it might be covered 'in depth' for 20 minutes or so in any given news hour on a 24/7 channel. This means more angles and more commentary, with reputations on the line for increased time periods. A serious crisis – a train crash or an oil spill for example – might result in almost blanket news coverage. For the company involved, this means no respite from the scrutiny. It also means that new angles to the story are likely to emerge, which in turn might lead the news agenda for all media.

Clearly, it is in the interest of 24/7 broadcast media in particular for stories to have staying power (or 'legs', so they can run and run). Conflict gives a story legs, and the best sort of conflict for a journalist is between what viewers, listeners or readers will see as 'good' and 'bad'. Perhaps we all miss the stories of our childhood because it is stories with victims, villains and heroes that are apparently most appealing to us. And, in issues and crisis management, the role normally filled by business is the one of villain.

The need for speed in news gathering, which comes from the competitive nature of the industry and the desire to be first with the news, has additional consequences for reputation management. In the rush to get something on air as quickly as possible, 24/7 news channels now report events as they experience them, rather than allowing themselves time to check facts and attempt any sort of analysis. 'Breaking news' is therefore as new to the newscasters as it is to the viewers, and phrases like 'reports are coming in of… ' and 'we're getting unconfirmed reports of… ' are commonplace. This might be followed by a live telephone conversation with someone who has either witnessed an event or who supposedly has some information about the developing story, but, again, such disclaimers as 'what we're hearing at the moment… ' will be used.[8] This increases the likelihood that an organization will find itself thrust into the limelight when only sketchy details of a crisis or issue are available. The organization may feel uncomfortable dealing with live media interviews when little is known about what has happened but, unless it engages with the media in these early moments of a crisis, it is possible that it will never regain the initiative.

Speed has also led to the developing phenomenon of citizen journalism. In a crisis, the need for a television news channel to broadcast pictures and eye witness accounts is overwhelming.

Depending on where the incident has happened, it might take some time to get a camera to the scene. Broadcast news channels may send 'scouts' on motorcycles to the scene of a physical crisis to assess the best potential camera shots whilst the more cumbersome outside broadcast units are rerouted, but this could still take hours. With many mobile telephones now able to take reasonable quality photographs or moving images, a source of instant visuals is at hand.

Within minutes of the 7/7 attacks on London, for example, the BBC and other news channels were receiving images from mobile phones. The BBC had 50 images within an hour and amassed thousands over the next few hours.[9] Six months later, the BBC received 6,500 e-mailed mobile images and video clips showing the spectacular fires at the Buncefield oil depot in Hertfordshire. One of the most telling stories I heard about Buncefield was from a professional photographer who said he was at the scene of the incident within 25 minutes. I thought he was telling me this as a matter of professional pride, but quite the opposite: 'I was way too late', he said, 'there were hundreds of decent amateur shots available on the internet before I even saw the flames.'

Up to now, television channels have relied on the 'citizen reporters' to contact them with their photos, videos and eye-witness accounts, but there are signs that the citizen reporting phenomenon might become formalized into a sort of wire service that receives, pays for and sells on photos and videos. Concerns about accuracy and fakes are currently few and far between, as there is little incentive for individuals to sensationalize. But, if money comes into the equation, these concerns may grow and organizations at the centre of a news story might have yet another dimension of media accuracy to worry about.

What about print media? On the face of it, the print media have not changed in news output for decades – there are still a handful of mainstream national newspapers in most countries publishing once a day. But behind the scenes, things have changed. For a start, all newspapers are now online as well as on hard copy, which means that their journalists are producing stories throughout the day. But perhaps the most important change that has happened is the increasing reliance on freelancers over staffers. This puts more pressure than ever on journalists to be good sellers because, if they don't sell their story to the editors, it might be cut down or cut out and they might not be paid for it. This encourages journalists to 'talk up' their stories, and this is often the root cause of what is called sensationalistic journalism.

One thing that reliably sells newspapers and pulls in the viewers and listeners is fear. This in turn is contributing to the zero risk culture in the developed world as discussed above. Health scares, food scares, contamination scares... all are lapped up by the consumers of media. So much so, that you occasionally get two seemingly opposing risks or fears being played out with almost no recognition by the media of its role in whipping up the fear frenzy. For example, the twin 'public health risks' of obesity and eating disorders. It seems that, if we're not being told that we are too fat, we are being told that our obsession with weight is causing eating disorders such as anorexia and bulimia in teenagers.

Of course, none of this matters if nobody believes what they read, see and hear in the media. Polls suggest that, in most countries, the media enjoy levels of trust even lower than businesses and governments. So perhaps we shouldn't worry too much.

Again, the polls are potentially misleading here. We may, as consumers of the modern media, be intellectually aware that the media are sensationalistic, or that the nature of the media is to provoke conflict, but although we have other sources of knowledge in this world of information, few of us bother to seek second opinions or to hear what has happened from the horse's mouth. How many times have you watched a television news piece overtly criticizing a company and thought: 'I wonder if that's true; I'll see what the company has to say on its website'? Very rarely, I suspect. If our opinion towards a company changes after it has been through a crisis or is in the midst of an issue, it is rarely because we have contacted the company ourselves to check the facts. It is because we see how the company is portrayed in the media and, importantly, how it has portrayed itself in the media.

Anyone who has ever run a media training session knows that most trainees are naturally sceptical of journalists. Participants will often recount a story of when their organization was last in the news, pointing out the factual errors made by journalists and accusing them of sensationalistic reporting. But, when asked to discuss other news stories about other organizations, the participants will normally accept how the media have portrayed the organizations involved. Most people do believe what they see, hear and read in the media... except when it is about them or their organization.

Today, organizations need to manage their reputations actively in the traditional media. That means being selective (as it is almost impossible to satisfy all media demands when reputation is under threat), confident, assertive and realistic. Understanding the media is fundamental to managing reputation. If you expect balanced reporting, you will be disappointed. But understand what they are looking for and who they are appealing to, and you have a fighting chance of getting a good share of voice and an opportunity to protect and enhance your reputation with your key audiences.

Online media

The traditional media is changing, but largely in response to the threat it perceives from online media. It is the internet that has really changed our way of looking for and receiving information, and organizations are still struggling to find their place and voice (and tone of voice) in this fast-developing forum.

Whilst it provides them with a powerful new tool for selling products and services, the internet also presents organizations with enormous reputation challenges. It is extremely difficult to fathom – unlike newspapers and broadcast networks, which are far more accountable (in most countries) and penetrable – and extremely difficult to control. It is essentially a sort of information anarchy, and we all know that companies and other organizations like structure and predictability.

The internet has become a powerful medium for anti-corporate messages. With posted material remaining live indefinitely, information becomes basically 'timeless'. If you 'Google' for Nike, you will be just one click away from the 'Boycott Nike' site. Type in Nestlé and you are just a step away from the Baby Milk Action site, which is dedicated to exposing what it sees as Nestlé's corporate irresponsibility. Add to this the umpteen blogs and the fact that one in every three teenagers is already generating online content, and the company's own official corporate website is suddenly just one of many voices battling for a share of voice about itself and its reputation. And of all the voices, perhaps the corporate voice is the least trusted.

Companies are trying to cope with this by engaging with this exciting new medium, and there are plenty of consultants there to help them get it right. But more than a little care is needed when an upstanding member of the global corporate community decides to defend or promote its reputation in this unregulated and risky new world. When I see companies like BP and McDonald's setting up 'blogs' or hosting discussion rooms about their businesses or brands, the picture that pops into my mind is one of middle-aged people trying to be 'down with the kids' and entering a world with which they are basically uncomfortable. Why do 'open forums' about brands help manage reputation, build trust or sell products? I see and hear the logical answers ('because these discussions happen anyway and you might as well have a voice in them...', 'because brands should be positioned as owned by consumers not companies... ' and so on) but the dynamics and practicalities of the internet present so many seemingly insurmountable difficulties, that it still seems like more of a risk than an opportunity.

Media trainers will tell you to focus on 'message, medium and audience', and the internet is not always the right medium to get your message across to your audience. A company must be accountable for what it says and does in terms of information provision, whereas ordinary internet users and professional corporate critics are not. It's an uncomfortable mismatch.

Googling for corporate giants

These are the sites found on the first page of Google results when the following company names are searched for:

Nestlé
http://www.nestle.co.uk (*UK corporate homepage*)
http://www.nestle.co.uk/careers (*careers section of corporate website*)
http://www.nestle.com (*global corporate homepage*)
http://www.babymilkaction.org/pages/boycott.html (*the 'Boycott Nestlé' page of anti-Nestlé campaign group Baby Milk Action*)
http://www.babymilkaction.org (*home page of anti-Nestlé campaign group Baby Milk Action*)
http://www.inminds.co.uk/boycott-nestle.html (*'Boycott Nestlé' page of Boycott Israel Campaign*)

http://en.wikipedia.org/wiki/Nestl%C3%A9 (*Nestlé section of the famous Wikipedia site*)

http://www.mcspotlight.org/beyond/nestle.html#nestle (*'Nestlé in the McSpotlight' page of the anti-McDonald's and anti-corporate website*)

http://www.booktrusted.co.uk/nestle (*Nestlé children's book prize*)

http://www.nestleusa.com (*US corporate homepage*)

McDonald's

http://www.mcdonald's.co.uk (*McDonald's UK corporate website*)

http://www.mcdonald's.com (*McDonald's corporate website*)

http://www.mcspotlight.org/case/index.html (*website for anti-McDonald's/'McLibel' trial groups*)

http://en.wikipedia.org/wiki/McDonald%E2%80%99s (*McDonald's web page on Wikipedia website*)

http://www.inminds.co.uk/boycott-mcdonalds.html (*'Boycott McDonald's' web page from Boycott Israel website*)

http://www.mcvideogame.com (*anti-McDonald's video game*)

http://www.mcdonalds.ca/en/index.aspx (*Canadian McDonald's corporate website*)

www.metro.co.uk/news/article.html?in_article_id=26183&in_page_id=34 (*news article from the Metro paper concerning McDonald's patenting method for making certain sandwiches*)

http://www.mwr.org.uk/home.htm (*website for McDonald's Workers' Resistance, global unofficial network of McDonald's employees that pursue an anti-McDonald's agenda*)

Starbucks

http://starbucks.co.uk/en-GB/ (*Starbucks UK website*)

http://www.starbucks.co.uk/en-GB/_Social+Responsibility (*Starbucks UK Corporate Social Responsibility web page*)

http://www.starbucks.com (*Starbucks corporate website*)

http://www.starbucks.com/retail/locator/default.aspx (*Starbucks store locator web page*)

http://en.wikipedia.org/wiki/Starbucks (*Starbucks page from Wikipedia website*)

http://www.inminds.co.uk/boycott-starbucks.html (*'Boycott Starbucks' web page from Boycott Israel website*) http://starbucksgossip.typepad.com/ (*blog covering Starbucks-related news; positive and negative coverage*)

http://www.spacehijackers.co.uk/starbucks/index.html (*web page for 'We Hate Starbucks' campaign*)

http://www.starbucks.ca/en-ca/ (*Starbucks Canadian website*)

http://news.bbc.co.uk/2/hi/uk_news/6086330.stm (*BBC news story detailing allegations of Starbucks withholding profits from Ethiopian farmers*)

Coca-Cola

http://www.coca-cola.com/glp/d/index-d.html (*corporate website for the Coca-Cola Company*)

http://www.coca-cola.co.uk (*UK corporate website for the Coca-Cola Company*)

http://www.coca-cola.co.uk/football (*corporate sponsorship page for UEFA European 2008 football championship*)

http://www.cokecce.co.uk/cce/index.jsp (*UK corporate website for Coca-Cola distribution network*)

http://en.wikipedia.org/wiki/Coca-Cola (*Coca-Cola section of Wikipedia website*)

http://www.waronwant.org/downloads/cocacola.pdf (*alternative company report from the War on Want anti-globalization NGO*)

http://sport.independent.co.uk/football/coca_cola (The Independent *newspaper's coverage of English Coca-Cola-sponsored football league*)

http://www.football-league.premiumtv.co.uk/page/Home/0,,10794,00.html (*website of the English football league, sponsored by Coca-Cola*)

http://www.inminds.co.uk/boycott-coca-cola.html (*'Boycott Coca-Cola' web page of Boycott Israel website*)

Exxon

http://www.exxon.com/USA-English/gFM/home_Contact_Us/homepage.asp (*Exxon corporate website*)

http://www.exxonmobil.com/corporate/ (*ExxonMobil corporate website*)

http://www.exxonmobil.co.uk/UK-English/uk_homepage.asp (*ExxonMobil UK corporate website*) http://en.wikipedia.org/wiki/Exxon (*Exxon section of Wikipedia website*)

http://en.wikipedia.org/wiki/Exxon_Valdez (*Exxon Valdez* incident section of Wikipedia website)

http://www.exxonsecrets.org (*anti-ExxonMobil organization website*)

http://www.exxposeexxon.com (*website for the Exxpose Exxon campaign*)

http://technorati.com/tag/Exxon (*list of blogs discussing Exxon from the Technorati blog search website*)

http://www.exxonmobilchemical.com/public_Siteflow/ WorldwideEnglish/ChemicalHomePage.asp (*ExxonMobil Chemicals division corporate website*)

http://www.evostc.state.ak.us (*website for* Exxon Valdez *Oil Spill Trustee Council*)

Googling done in the United Kingdom on 11 June 2007.

Some companies are also jumping on the e-mail bandwagon as a way to 'engage' directly with consumers and other stakeholders. Again, this needs very careful management. On two recent occasions, the company I run has been called in to help in emerging confrontations between small action groups and big businesses. On both occasions, to our astonishment, the Chief Executive was in regular e-mail contact with the head of the action group. In both cases, the Chief Executive thought he was doing the right thing by replying almost instantly (certainly on the same day) to questions and demands made by the action group: 'I thought direct engagement with stakeholders was the done thing'. But all it had achieved was an empowered but unaccountable and unrepresentative action group, an escalated issue, a marginalized set of genuine customers and stakeholders and a workload that no chief executive should need to worry about.

The world of information anarchy is here to stay, but it needs careful management. There are no universal answers to the problems it can cause, but quality and quantity are the key variables. Better information is preferable to just more information, both for the company and its intended audience.

Individuals are empowered

In a book about corporate reputation, for 'individuals' we could perhaps substitute 'consumers', right? Wrong.

Not every individual who feels that they have a stake in a company's reputation might be a consumer of that company's goods or services. If McDonald's only had to worry about individuals who were regular consumers of its hamburgers, the company would probably find corporate reputation a whole lot easier to manage. The fact is that there are individuals who, through clever use of the other players (particularly NGOs and the media), make it their business to oppose the company's plans, policies and existence, whether or not they have ever even been inside a McDonald's. The difference between 'consumer activism' and 'individual activism' is extremely important, because it gives companies a dilemma: do we give our consumers what they really want, what they say they want, or what others want them to want?

What do consumers want? By definition, consumers want something. Once they have decided that they want something – whether it is a holiday, a hamburger, a cure for an ailment, an hour of legal advice, a pension policy or anything else – they look at who is available to provide them with that product or service. Assuming there is a choice, the three main factors influencing their consumption decision are personal taste, price and quality.

Is this what they say they want? If you believe the media, and/or if you believe everyone tells the truth all the time in surveys, you will think that people are increasingly making choices using factors other than these. But there is a difference between what people say and what people do. So whilst the statement that 'more and more of us are making ethical purchasing decisions' might be true, companies look at the sales figures rather than the newspapers to see the extent of the change. The percentage of consumers who actually make a choice based primarily on ethical or social factors may indeed be growing, but it is still only a very small number.

And what do others want them to want? This is where the difference between consumer and individual comes in to play. Some people want to boycott non-fair trade coffee and persuade all coffee companies to adopt what they see as fair trade policies; they want no one to drive SUVs because they are environmentally irresponsible;

they want all companies to invest in good causes. Some people call this 'consumer activism', but it is actually social and economic activism that is directed at companies. This is healthy human behaviour in the free market, but it is different from being a consumer. It is about being an empowered individual.

Back to the corporate dilemma: do we give our consumers products based on the agendas of others, do we give them products based on what surveys seem to suggest they want, or do we give them what buying patterns actually show us they want? Sometimes, you hear companies saying things like: 'What our consumers are telling us is that they want more responsible products' and 'Our customers really care about our positioning on key social issues.' But whatever companies say in public, they know that their consumers still primarily want products and services based on personal taste, cost and quality.

This difference between what is said and what is done can create a reputation minefield and is at the heart of allegations made against companies that are 'not going far enough' in addressing 'consumer concerns'. In fact, it is rarely 'consumer concerns' that are not being addressed; it is the concerns of the empowered individual and campaign groups who are making a difference through successful use of the media and other stakeholders.

A few years ago, businesses were all on the lookout for the NGO that might spot a problem or escalate an issue. Developments in communication technologies coupled with the needs of the modern media mean that now any individual – member of staff, customer, neighbour, or even just an individual with an opinion – potentially has this power.

A uniform uniform policy?

An example of the power of the individual to effect change is the story of an employee facing up to British Airways about the right to wear a religious symbol. In October 2006, British Airways employee Nadia Eweida received much media coverage after BA bosses told her she could not wear a cross over her uniform while performing her job as a check-in agent at Heathrow Airport. Having worn her cross for the previous seven years of employment, Ms Eweida refused to comply with the policy and declined the offer of a new (non-public-facing) position in which she did not have to cover the cross. Placed on unpaid leave, Ms Eweida said she planned to sue the airline for religious discrimination. Christian groups accused British Airways of double standards, as Sikh and Muslim employees were not prevented from wearing religious symbols (garments) to work. The airline's uniform policy was apparently not applied in a uniform fashion.

The issue emerged for BA at a time when symbols of religious 'difference' were high on the UK media's agenda, thanks to a debate sparked by a former home secretary about Muslim women wearing full veils in public. Nadia Eweida was thus extremely hot media property. There were plenty of media people on hand to ensure that her story was heard and the issue debated.

As the salience of the issue grew, BA drew criticism from significant religious groups and was even faced with a possible boycott and a threat from the Church of England to rid itself of its £10.25 million shares in the airline if it didn't retreat and instigate a formal review of uniform guidelines. Even the Prime Minister stepped in to the debate, advising the airline to do the 'sensible thing'.

BA remained resolute throughout that it was simply enforcing its own policy on uniforms that had been in place for many years. But this technocratic message was no match for the emotional argument that Ms Eweida and her growing band of advocates were using. BA belatedly realized that it was in a no-win situation and that it had to close the issue off with actions, not words. The company announced a review of its 34-page uniform policy, adding that it had been 'unfairly accused' of being anti-Christian. On 19 January 2007, BA announced that it would in future allow employees to wear a symbol of faith on a lapel pin, 'with some flexibility ... to wear a symbol of faith on a chain'.

NGOs are empowered

Few could dispute that the big 'winners' in recent decades have been NGOs. They are increasingly influential, filling our airwaves and newspapers, and enjoy favourable trust ratings compared with the media, governments and business in most countries.

It is hard to find a business person who doesn't have a strong view on the influence and tactics of NGOs. Some see them as an excellent conduit to other stakeholders and possible partners in good business initiatives; others see them as unhelpful and unaccountable agitators who attack business unfairly to further their own narrow agendas. The right answer is that they are both. Some are certainly worth engaging and working with; others are not.

The term 'international NGO' was first used during the establishment of the UN and was defined in 1950 as 'any international organization that is not founded by an international treaty'.[10] This was an effort to describe organizations such as the International Red Cross and Red Crescent, which do good work and are worthy of special recognition, as a special category. Statistics tell us that there are now more than 2 million NGOs in the United States alone, and that there are 40,000 NGOs that can legitimately be called international.[11] Not all of them are as worthy of special recognition as the Red Cross.

So, when a company asks itself: 'What is our policy on engaging NGOs?', it is asking the wrong question.

It seems that almost all groups of people with a shared interest or a shared standpoint can be classed as an NGO, from the local scout troop to the international environmental campaign movement. Is Oxfam an NGO? Or is it a charity? Or both? Is Greenpeace an NGO or a lobby group? In many ways, the name shouldn't matter, but it does seem odd having the Society for the Preservation of Beers from the Wood, the World Association for the School as an Instrument of Peace and the Infernal Noise Brigade in the same category on the stakeholder engagement list as the Red Cross.

The power of NGOs comes partly from their 'independent' status and the perception that they are staffed with people who are 'more ordinary' than governments, businesses and the media. The truth is that most NGOs are very partial, staffed with the same sort of people as any other organization, unelected and unaccountable except to their members. In many respects, they are like businesses: they have priorities, incomings and outgoings, agendas and customers. The global lobby groups and charities are huge professional businesses in their own right, with massive advertising budgets and aggressive campaigns. Greenpeace, for example, has an income of over US$130 million a year. But it is still perceived as the 'underdog' or even the 'hero' in the media.

A major source of NGOs' power is the role that they perform for the media in providing comment and conflict. An illustration of this comes from the oil industry: when Shell announced its profits in 2005, there was significant negative coverage in the UK media. *The Daily Express* ran a story on 3 February under the headline 'Motorists Protest at Shell's £13bn Profits'. The piece stated that 'the firm came under attack from consumer groups and environmentalists' and went on to quote various people: the Chairperson of the Fuel Lobby (concerned about tax-paying motorists), a spokesperson from the Road Haulage Association (concerned about the haulage industry), the General Secretary of the Amicus Union (concerned about pensioners' home heating costs), a spokesperson from a price comparison and supplier switching service (concerned that it is not only motorists but also householders paying high costs to generate profits), the General Secretary of the Transport and General Workers Union (calling for a windfall tax) and Friends of the Earth (concerned about climate change and human rights). Six NGOs (if the unions are allowed to be included as NGOs, which I think they are in this context at least) quoted in one 700-odd word article, and all critical of a company that is generating huge amounts of wealth for UK PLC.

None of the above should be taken as a value judgement about NGOs. There is no doubt in my mind that a pluralist world is a good thing, and that many NGOs have made major contributions – with or without business partnerships – to important local, national and global issues. I just happen to think that the way businesses treat NGOs is often naive. 'Conflict' groups in particular are given too much respect, partly because they are lumped in the same category as potential valued partners such as charities and genuinely representative community groups.

The idea that to be a good business you need to react to the agendas of some of these NGOs and 'do something' in partnership with them is ludicrous and will possibly lead to more problems than solutions. One corporate affairs manager said to me recently: 'We listened to the environmental NGOs and we made changes and we even got them in to play a role as a partner; they then turned around to the media and said the changes were corporate greenwash.' This is because, as Judy Larkin has written, 'activists deal with problems; companies deal with issues', the difference being that a company can address an issue with a view to finding a solution, whilst activists see that the wider problem still exists and blame the company for not doing more.[12]

Part of the problem is that communications people often use the wrong language with business people on NGO 'engagement'. The idea of partnering with an NGO can make some business people fall over with fear, as the image that they have in mind when they think 'NGO' is one of the well-known activist groups. New language might help separate these groups in people's minds, and help them see that partnering with a reliable and genuinely representative community group might in fact keep the larger activist groups at bay whilst making a real difference to a project or issue and even to the success of the business.

The book returns to this theme later on. For now, suffice it to say that the small world, the free world, the world of information and the world of fear is also the world of the NGO.

Governments remain powerful, whilst corporate power is waning

Despite the growth in numbers and powers of NGOs, governments remain the real powerhouses. The conventional wisdom might be that governments' powers have waned in the era of globalization, but this is overstated. Businesses and NGOs and individuals may lobby, and use the media to do so effectively, but governments still decide.

A 2007 report by the Hansard Society in the United Kingdom found that some MPs were being approached by lobbyists at least 100 times a week. It found that 59 per cent of MPs were contacted by interest groups at least 20 times a week. 51 per cent of MPs said they were lobbied at least 20 times a week by charities and 39 per cent said businesses lobbied them 20 times a week. In its report, entitled *Friend or Foe? Lobbying in British Democracy*, the Hansard Society described lobbying as 'symbolic of a healthy pluralistic democracy' in contrast with those who thought it was 'antithetical to democracy'.[13]

The first point to note on this is that, if the Hansard Society report is to be believed, politicians are lobbied more by interest groups and charities than by business. This might be against the conventional wisdom that lobbying is something slightly murky and underhand done primarily by wealthy businesses. The second point to note is that the very act of lobbying itself shows where the power lies:

You only have to visit a couple of smart-but-not-lavish restaurants within walking distance of every Congress, Parliament or National Assembly building in the world to see which side the bread is buttered... Does anyone suppose that corporations pay exorbitant fees to armies of lobbyists for the sheer hell of it, or because they like wasting money, or because they want to keep these restaurants in business? Or is it because they know where power truly lies: with elected governments, precisely where it should be?[14]

Although governments still have the power, they are struggling to retain control over certain global trends and issues. National efforts to address global issues such as poverty, climate change and mass migration can sometimes seem parochial and piecemeal, whilst inter-governmental efforts are frustratingly slow and inadequate.

This puts more pressure on companies, which are perceived to be the real sources of wealth and power in the era of globalization. Many people genuinely believe, for example, that oil companies were behind the Iraq war. Some think that billions of dollars of oil money were being poured into the re-election or even personal financial accounts of Washington and London politicians to ensure Iraq was 'captured' for its oil reserves. Most intelligent people know that this allegation is frankly ridiculous and insulting, but others clearly perceive the oil industry as the media presents it: rich men in ten-gallon hats who want to make money at the expense of the environment and don't care who dies and suffers along the way.

Furthermore, both consumers and individuals are extremely demanding of businesses. In some countries, the public has for some years placed taxing expectations on politicians – we demand much more of them than we do of ourselves. This is particularly true in the United States and the United Kingdom, where politicians need to be almost superhuman, devoid of any character failing. The same is starting to apply to businesses. We do not tolerate businesses getting things wrong even though, if we thought about it, a business is just a group of individuals who are as prone to mistakes and failings as we are.

Companies are important and powerful, but not nearly as important and powerful as the popular image of them might suggest. The idea that business is all-powerful and dictates to government is so far from the truth that it seems pointless wasting time challenging it. I have known chief executives and their helpers planning for weeks ahead of meetings with the lowliest of ministers, and the planning is certainly not on the lines of: 'We'll tell him to do this.' It's more: 'We need to show him that we understand his agenda and we can help him achieve it.' I am constantly surprised at how *lacking* in power businesses actually are when it comes to public issues. But perhaps some people just want to believe that there is a secret society of politicians and business people running the world from a Swiss mountain hideaway.

The new world order described above provides huge opportunities for businesses, but also increased scrutiny and risks. Corporate reputations are now on the line every minute of every day, not just when something goes wrong. Indeed, just posting a healthy profit now needs a reputation management strategy: 'Bad news, everyone, we have an issue: we made record profits this year. We'll be all over the news, with all manner of people criticizing us.' A former BBC journalist I know says that, for the purposes of creating stories, there are two types of companies: good companies and bad companies. The bad companies are big, profitable companies. The good companies are small, struggling companies.

One of the key themes of this book is that businesses have dealt with the new world order by keeping a relatively low profile on some of the key global challenges. They are generally wary of taking a stand or doing anything that might provoke confrontation. They understandably think that a strategy of 'as little media as possible on these issues' is the path of least resistance. They want to find solutions, build bridges, find partnerships and move forward in a stable and predictable way. Their starting point on most issues is to engage with the agendas of governments and NGOs, to seek out common ground and try to make a difference at the margins rather than to oppose. But companies are often alone in this conflict-avoidance strategy. It is often in the interests of the other players to provoke and sustain conflict, to blame, to demand and to ridicule. Conflict on issues is in the perceived interests of governments (who need it to provide differentiation and to impose their own solutions), NGOs and individuals (who need it to highlight causes) and the media (who need it for stories).

To the outside world, it perhaps looks like companies are intent on preserving the status quo. This then reinforces the image of companies as obstacles to progress, and sometimes they are. Companies can get it hopelessly wrong. Sometimes they get it wrong through greed or negligence, for which they should certainly be held to account. But mostly they get it wrong by accident because companies are as susceptible to human error as governments, the media, NGOs and individuals.

Tomorrow's world

Tomorrow's world, for companies, is an almost permanent reputational collision course. The old risks are still there, but added to them there are new risks. Companies now need to be prepared for the following reputation risks:

- Crises affecting them – asymmetric major shocks, such as a factory fire, an oil spill or a corporate governance scandal.
- Crises affecting a sector or wider group – such as terrorist attacks on infrastructure, or a health alert on a product that is sold by more than one company.
- Global societal issues – the big ones, such as global warming, obesity, child labour and fair trade.
- Corporate or performance-related issues – product quality, supply chain and corporate governance issues, for example.
- Local issues with possible wider consequences – these are the more parochial issues, where only a small element of society is affected, but which can still provoke a sense of injustice on a wider scale if managed poorly (a local health scare, contamination, facility closure and so on).
- Attacks on the basis of the company and its very existence – fast food companies, oil companies, coffee houses and others are all aware that they do not need to be experiencing a crisis or managing an issue to be under the reputation spotlight. This is closely connected with the CSR agenda.

This chapter started with an analysis of the financial services industry and the challenges it faces in the new external climate. Another industry that has had its reputation risk world turned on its head over the past few decades is the airline industry.

Turbulent times for the airlines

Airlines have always operated in an industry that has very high risks, but the past few years have seen the risks change. Twenty years ago, I suspect the 'risk register' for most airlines would have been heavily focused on plane crashes and strikes. Terrorist attacks on airlines (perhaps the most famous of which was the Pan Am disaster of 1988, in which 270 people died in the bombing of Flight 103), changed that. Crashes were no longer just about pilot or mechanical error; the threat of terrorism had added a new dimension. This took an even more fearsome turn in September 2001, when US airlines were hijacked and used as suicide missiles against key targets in New York and Washington.

Added to the terrorist threat are various other new reputation risks for airlines. Deep vein thrombosis, also known as 'economy class syndrome', emerged as an issue in late 2000 and, although the risk of getting DVT was estimated at 1 in 2.5 million,[15] it needed extremely careful communication and management by the airlines in the litigious world of zero tolerance to risk.

Passenger rights legislation, health and safety issues, fear of pandemic diseases, new cargo and hand baggage restrictions and disability access are all potential flashpoints that airlines must manage. But perhaps the biggest of the new reputation risks is environmental damage. The airline industry is being targeted as the fastest-growing contributor to climate change, and taxation both on airlines and their passengers is being implemented or considered in many countries.

British Airways in particular has had a painful few years in terms of reputation management, and is struggling to regain trust with its consumers and stakeholders. The causes of its troublesome recent past have been the conflict with one of its staff over the wearing of a religious symbol, the alleged involvement of senior staff members in price fixing with other airlines, a strike by staff of one of its suppliers (airline food manufacturers Gate Gourmet), which spread to BA staff, its handling of the government-imposed restrictions on hand baggage due to security concerns and its poor record in lost luggage.

All of the above has resulted in negative media coverage, which stresses that BA's reputation has been hit hard. During the strikes, for instance, *The Times* leader said that 'at the height of the holiday season, BA's reputation and its earnings have been badly hit'[16] and *The Daily Telegraph* stated that the strike 'will also damage the reputation of an airline which, for the third August in a row, has had to deal with massive disruption at the height of the holiday season'.[17] In a feature piece, *The Times* said: 'These strikes have done cumulative damage to the reputation of BA. The management deserves its share of blame. Difficult as its situation is, it seems on each occasion to have been taken by surprise. It lacks robust back-up systems.'[18]

After the allegations of price fixing, *The Business* newspaper asserted that 'BA's response to the OFT investigation into alleged price fixing … has damaged BA's standing in the world with customers, competitors, suppliers and staff... To suspend your commercial director and director of PR suggests guilt. It also smacks of panic. And it is extremely cackhanded PR.'[19]

Most major airlines are well prepared for a crisis, at least in theory. The vast majority of major airlines put their staff through regular exercises to test both the operational and the communications response to an accident or incident. Crashes are, thankfully, rare – although the busy skies suggest they might not be so rare in the future. But this does not mean that reputations are not challenged. Airlines are now far more likely to find their reputations dragged through the media for other issues such as those mentioned above. They need to ensure that their organizations are as well-equipped to cope with the new threats as they are with the old.

Summary

Changing external realities mean that companies no longer have to be in the midst of a crisis or even managing a developing issue to face a reputation threat. Risks are more immediate and public than they have ever been before. The balance of power between different players has changed, with more demanding customers and empowered individuals and groups. So no wonder companies are so often on the back foot; no wonder they sometimes feel unloved; and no wonder they are taking reputation management seriously.

Some commentators look at these developments and urge companies to engage with and fit in to the agendas of the other players, to go with the flow and build dialogue around common ground. But I think companies need to take a stronger line, to be more confident, assertive and combative when they are under fire and to take more of a leadership role during 'peacetime'. If they don't, they risk being the bullied child at school. The more the bullies feel that the child is weak and passive, the more they will bully. I suppose this book is the concerned parent saying: 'You don't have to take this any more! You are just as good as the other kids! You have to stand up for yourself!'

A passive, conflict-avoiding, stakeholder-pleasing stance on reputation management won't work within this new climate of perpetual reputation risk. So how can companies regain the reputation initiative?

Notes

1. *The Daily Telegraph* (22 November 2006) 'Golden Vacuum Award Tries to Say a Cleaner's Life Sucks'.
2. Norberg, J (2003) *In Defense of Global Capitalism*, Cato Institute, Washington, p 51.
3. BBC Online (24 November 2005) 'Chinese Papers Condemn Harbin "lies" '.
4. Interestingly, when one of my colleagues was managing the media response function during a recent client crisis, a journalist called from China. After a short exchange, the journalist asked: 'Is any of what you are saying true, or is it all just lies?' There is perhaps a mistrust of authorities (companies included) that will take a long time to change.
5. For a comprehensive and interesting discussion on changing attitudes to risk and recommended approaches for communicating risk, see Larkin, J (2003) *Strategic Reputation Risk Management*, Palgrave Macmillan, Basingstoke (especially Chapters 3 and 5).
6. See, for example, Institute of Business Ethics (February 2007) *Ethics Briefing: Surveys on Business Ethics* (4).
7. Mike Seymour (September 2004) 'Fighting On All Fronts', *CEO Magazine*, advertorial.
8. I should note that the BBC has implemented a clear policy of 'accuracy over speed' since the Hutton inquiry criticized its journalistic standards in 2004.
9. *The Guardian* (11 July 2005) 'We Had 50 Images Within An Hour'.
10. Resolution 288 (X) of ECOSOC on 27 February 1950.

11. LSE Centre for Civil Society and Centre for the Study of Global Governance (2001) *Global Civil Society 2001*, Oxford University Press, New York.
12. Larkin, J (2003) *Strategic Reputation Risk Management*, Palgrave Macmillan, Basingstoke, p 151.
13. Hansard Society (2007) *Friend or Foe? Lobbying in British Democracy*. Available at http://www.hansardsociety.org.uk/node/view/773. Accessed on: 11 June 2007.
14. Hilton, S and Gibbons, G (2002) *Good Business*, Texere, London, p 48.
15. Kraaijenhagen, RA, Haverkamp, D, Koopman, MM, Prandoni, P, Piovella, F and Büller, HR (2000) Travel and risk of venous thrombosis, *The Lancet*, **356** (9240).
16. *The Times* (13 August 2005), 'Attitude Sickness; British Airways Cannot Afford Another Summer of Strikes'.
17. *The Daily Telegraph* (13 August 2005), 'BA Picks up the Pieces as Wildcat Action Strands 113,000 People Across the World'.
18. *The Times* (15 August 2005), 'Arthur Scargill Flies Again'.
19. *The Business* (2 July 2006), 'Walsh Flies BA into a Public Relations Disaster'.

3 Regaining the reputation initiative

Do you ever feel that you're damned if you do and damned if you don't? In this new perpetual collision course of reputation management, many organizations would be forgiven for feeling they are.

I have recently had conversations with various corporate executives who are realizing that, whichever way they turn and whatever they do and advocate, there is a vociferous lobby criticizing them and using the increasingly hostile (traditional and online) media to do so. Conflict is the order of the day, and reputations are under threat on an almost permanent basis. So how can companies start to turn this around?

The previous chapter argued that there is occasionally some naivety in how companies engage with stakeholders on the many new issues that face them today. One question that I think companies sometimes fail to ask is this: Before we engage with the developing agenda on this matter (whether it is a local, national or international issue that we have identified as a potential reputation threat), and before we start to think of initiatives we can undertake to show that we are willing to adapt and learn, what exactly are the people who are opposing us or demanding something of us trying to achieve?

One very local example: in my neighbourhood in North London, a supermarket proposed to build a new store towards the end of the high street. The supermarket, Waitrose, is perceived to be a fairly upmarket store and in many areas is welcomed as a sign of increasing neighbourhood affluence. In this case, however, a local campaign group led by local retailers and calling itself 'Warning on Waitrose' (WOW) popped up and led a successful campaign against the planning application. Their argument was that the new store would have a detrimental effect on the 'local independent' high street shops, and would ultimately undercut their prices and put them out of business.

Rewind now to about 10 years ago when, in many parts of the United Kingdom, there was outrage about supermarkets building new 'out-of-town' or 'off-high-street' stores. These, it was argued, would encourage people to get in their cars and drive to shop for groceries. This unnecessary car use would be environmentally damaging and would discourage people from using their 'local independent' high street shops. Instead, campaigners wanted money to be invested in our high streets, so they could be developed and turned into thriving commercial centres again.

It seemed to me at the time of the more recent proposals that the same people who campaigned against off-high-street supermarket development some years ago were now campaigning against on-high-street supermarket development. Clearly, the campaigners can't have it both ways. Or can they? Did Waitrose ever ask itself this: 'What exactly are the people who oppose us trying to achieve?'

The answer is not just that local opponents want to protect local businesses, or that they want to protect the environment. This is part of the equation, but not the whole. It is simply this: most of the opponents do not like Waitrose. They do not like any supermarkets. They probably do not like profitable companies at all. They have a vision of what their neighbourhood should look like and where their neighbours should shop and this vision excludes the likes of Waitrose. Their views may therefore seem contradictory (no high street development; no out-of-town development) but in fact, they are completely consistent: no development by supermarkets at all. They are absolutely entitled to this view, but it is not the view of the less vocal majority, most of whom would probably quite like a convenient, inexpensive and efficient supermarket on their doorstep rather than having to drive a few miles to find one or pay higher prices on the high street.

What follows is often a hard pill for companies to swallow, but it is necessary to get it out in the open clearly and unequivocally. Sensitive corporate people should look away now, as this section contains harsh news:

- Some people do not like you.
- Some people want you to fail.
- Some people do not want to seek solutions to issues that they and you have identified.
- Some people do not want to find common ground. Whatever you do, they will find a way to criticize you.

But do not worry; do not take this to heart. It is fine to have opponents. You will never be all things to all people.

What does this mean for dealing with WOW and the many similar groups that exist at all levels and in all countries? Should companies always 'engage with their agenda' or 'seek common ground' or try to 'allay their concerns'?

In the more recent case, Waitrose did everything that PR people always suggest: it held a public meeting for example, to 'hear the concerns' of local residents. It looked at the 'associated issues' with store development, trying to find solutions to local traffic increases and concerns about effects on the local green spaces. It did everything except take on its opponents on the substance of the main debate: whether or not it is good to have a supermarket on the high street.

Most companies, in my experience, do the same. They are not in a position to manage the new world order. They are reactive, cumbersome organizations that want to keep as low a profile as possible on key issues for fear of unwanted publicity. They may talk the language of reputation, but they have a limited number of tools at their disposal to manage it. They are often so blinkered by the fear of big crises that they do not see that they are experiencing reputation threats almost every day. They seem to accept that business is seen as bad by the outside world and that it is the agendas of others that lead important debates.

This all leads potentially to a downward reputation spiral. It means that, despite all the brochures that companies have produced, all the crises they have managed well, all the standards they have signed up to and all the money they have invested in social initiatives, none of this seems to shield them from the bad times.

What I believe is that companies like Waitrose should stand up for what they believe is right, have confidence that their plans will be popular and represent progress and development, show that they will be a good corporate citizen in the neighbourhood, galvanize the silent majority who are broadly supportive of development and do battle with opponents in the public domain if need be. And if this puts reputations on the line and creates publicity, so be it. Reputations are on the line already.

I am not the first person to advocate courageous steps to change this negative worldview of companies. Todd Stitzer, Chief Executive of Cadbury Schweppes, wrote an excellent call to action in the *Financial Times* in June 2006. In the article, entitled 'Business Must Loudly Proclaim What It Stands For', he writes: 'Business is not truly trusted and the sad fact is that to a great extent we only have ourselves to blame. This is not because we have actually committed evil, but because we have allowed others to characterize our actions and our motives, while we have been focused on doing business.' He goes on to note that 'the distrust has become so entrenched that rather than reach out, many companies have retreated and not communicated, fearing what people will say and what journalists will write'.[1] Stitzer's conclusions, that this is 'a counsel of despair that cannot continue' and that business can no longer afford to pursue a policy of invisibility, is essentially what I mean when I say that business must 'regain the reputation initiative'.

This chapter looks at three big picture changes that can be made, before the rest of the book focuses on what this means in terms of specific changes that can help companies better manage their reputations in the areas of crisis management, issues management and CSR. The three changes in this section are:

- changing the corporate mindset;
- putting reputation at the heart of the business;
- redrawing the corporate stakeholder engagement map.

Changing the corporate mindset

As Todd Stitzer suggests, the key change is a change in the corporate mindset, from passive and apologetic to confident, assertive and (where required) combative. I would suggest that the mindset that the corporate world has today is as follows:

The world outside is a tough one, with many stakeholders portraying us in the corporate world as evil capitalists treading over everyone's rights and opportunities to get whatever we want. There is some truth in this – we do enjoy wealth in a world that is blighted by poverty and inequality. We should therefore change our ways, show that we are willing to learn and engage and address the concerns that our stakeholders have. However, the ultimate goal is to keep a low profile on these issues and, as long as we are ready to face major crises in our organization, we should be able to shield ourselves from the worst threats to our reputation.

And I think we need to get to here:

The world outside is a tough one, with many stakeholders portraying us in the corporate world as evil capitalists treading over everyone's rights and opportunities to get whatever we want. But that's just not true. We are proud of where we are and what we stand for, and we have reached where we are because we have served our customers well. We believe we can contribute to a positive future for the world, in the same way that we have led progress in the past. We are not perfect, but with the talents and people we have, we are normally on top of the bigger issues we face. We must not be complacent, as we are staffed with people who are as susceptible to human error and misjudgement as anyone else. On key issues, we have a voice that matches our status and contribution, and we do not allow others to dominate the agenda. If we do, we run the risk that our reputation will be determined by the perceptions of a few rather than by the realities that we and our customers experience.

Whilst the media regularly portrays business as being powerful and influential, I think it is actually surprising how infrequently big businesses are seen to be speaking out on significant issues that affect them. When businesses do speak out on issues, it is now increasingly seen as an 'intervention'. It is as if the prevailing climate has turned against business so much that it is now unacceptable for companies that create wealth and jobs and keep pension funds afloat to have a voice.

There have been some interesting cases recently in which companies have taken the initiative, had a strong voice on major issues and managed the inevitable interest in this 'intervention'.

TOTAL outrage

The French oil giant TOTAL became a political football in the 2007 French presidential elections. When the company announced net profits for 2006 of £8.4 billion – the largest ever for a French company – socialist candidate Ségolène Royal called for a windfall tax on petrol profits to pay for public transport and home insulation. Leading conservative candidate Nicolas Sarkozy responded to the profit announcement by suggesting that TOTAL should cut petrol prices at the pump. I can well imagine the sorts of conversations that this generated in TOTAL's group headquarters:

'If we enter this debate, we risk giving the story legs. Let's just stay out of it and watch it blow over.'

'But surely we should not allow the politicians to use the success of our company to further their own agendas?'

'They will move on to something else soon. The best we can do is wait for the agenda to change.'

The path of least resistance for TOTAL would have been to sit tight and wait for the debate to wane, hoping that neither of the candidates would actually turn their electoral posturing into policy once elected. But TOTAL decided to defend itself. This was a risky strategy, as the French company had experienced various high-profile crises in the preceding few years: the *Erika* oil spill off the coast of Brittany, the Toulouse factory disaster and the arrest of its Chief Executive for his alleged role in the oil for food scandal. TOTAL would have been excused for keeping its head down.

However, Thierry Desmarest, TOTAL's outgoing Chief Executive responded to the political debate by saying that Ségolène Royal's idea was demagogic, populist and dogmatic. This was echoed by his successor Christophe de Margerie who said: 'In a country where people find it indecent to make profits, there is a time when you need to know what you want. If you want to keep big French groups capable of battling internationally, you must not shoot them in the back.'[2] A corporate ally emerged in the form of Daniel Bouton, Chief Executive of French bank Société Générale, who warned that 'if this country prefers mediocrity, that [the policies espoused by the presidential candidates] is what we should have'.[3]

The result was that the debate quickly moved on. Many newspapers carried the politicians' suggestions and few carried TOTAL's rebuttal, but the senior management's 'fightback' may have been enough to persuade the politicians to shy away from further confrontation. Politicians may thrive on conflict, but ultimately they cannot afford too many enemies.

Airtime for airlines

In the United Kingdom, the holiday group First Choice took a strong line on the government's air duty increases. In the pre-Budget report announced in December 2006, the Treasury announced that it planned to double Air Passenger Duty on flights as part of its efforts to address the problem of carbon emissions.

Peter Long, Chief Executive of First Choice Holidays, led the criticism of the Treasury's decision. He branded it a 'stealth tax', claiming the rise in duty had nothing to do with carbon emissions and only served to bolster the government's coffers. First Choice threatened to drop its voluntary carbon emission match-funding scheme. The company's criticisms of government policy received significant coverage, making almost all UK national newspapers. It also encouraged others to follow suit, with Flybe calling the tax 'the poll tax of the skies' and Ryanair's Michael O'Leary (who needs little encouragement) running a series of advertisements attacking the Chancellor's 'tax grab'.

The government clearly felt that it had the upper hand in the debate (a green tax on wealthy airlines) and took the debate further. In an interview with left-leaning national UK newspaper *The Guardian*, the Environment Minister Ian Pearson criticized the airline industry for not pulling its weight in the fight against climate change. The Minister said that British Airways was 'only just playing ball' on environmental regulations, criticized Lufthansa and said the attitude of US airlines was 'a disgrace'. He saved the most severe criticism for Ryanair, which he described as 'not just the unacceptable face of capitalism, but also the irresponsible face of capitalism'. He went on to describe Ryanair Chairperson Michael O'Leary as 'completely off the wall'.[4]

Michael O'Leary hit back by saying his airline was 'the greenest in Europe' (as it has the newest fleet and operates at capacity more often than its competitors) and said Ian Pearson was 'silly' and 'hasn't a clue what he is talking about'. O'Leary said that Ryanair planes had cut their emissions and fuel consumption by 50 per cent over the previous five years. He added that the Minister should instead be attacking power stations and road transport, claiming they account for over 50 per cent of carbon emissions.

The media enjoyed the conflict, and came down on the side of the airlines. *The Sunday Times* said that the Minister's outburst was borne out of frustration at the government's failure to bring airlines into line on carbon emissions. *The Independent* shared a similar view: 'It's easier for him [Ian Pearson] to blame it all on Mr O'Leary, Lufthansa and British Airways than to risk a few votes by actually trying to do something about it.'[5]

Ian Pearson then had to endure various painfully embarrassing television interviews in which he was repeatedly urged to apologize, and it was widely reported that he was chastized by Environment Secretary David Milliband and other senior government ministers.

Emboldened by the fact that Ryanair had taken on the government on a green issue and won, in early 2007, just after the tax had taken effect, the Federation of Tour Operators said that it would mount a challenge at the High Court on the basis that the rise in Air Passenger Duty is illegal. The move was reported fairly neutrally by the media, with some taking the side of business against the government and few suggesting that the motivation of the airline industry was corporate greed.

Surveys still suggest, however, that the public does not believe the airline industry is doing enough to address global warming. A 'concerned consumer' survey in *The Times* shows that 35 per cent of people blame airlines for the environmental impact of flying (against 18 per cent for passengers, 18 per cent for government, 17 per cent for aircraft-makers and 13 per cent for oil companies). The same survey shows that 60 per cent of passengers would fly less frequently to help reduce greenhouse gas emissions, 'but only if there were no other way of solving the environmental impact of aviation'.[6] Consumers are not significantly changing their behaviour (we are taking more flights, not fewer), and are shifting the blame primarily to industry.

So, this 'fightback' by the airlines has met with mixed success and there is still a way to go if airlines are successfully going to defend their reputations in the global warming debate. But, even if the legal challenge is unsuccessful, the Treasury has been sent a clear message that the airline and holiday industry will not stand back and allow politicians to use climate change theory to impose regulations and taxes on the industry.

Other companies are changing their corporate mindsets too. GM head of global communications, Steve Harris, was given a full-page spread in the *Financial Times* in early 2007, entitled 'How GM Learnt to Speak Up For Itself'.[7] In the article, Harris explains the internal benefits of taking stronger external positions: 'When you get out there and stand up for yourself, this plays extremely well internally. Everybody wants to feel like we're not just going to take this lying down, we're going to fight back.' He goes on to recount a recent experience in which he took on a *New York Times* journalist, turning a piece of aggressive and (in his view) unfair journalism into a rallying call for staff and customers in certain parts of the United States.

Despite the fact that some companies show similar willingness to stand up and be counted, I still find that I say: 'Where are you?', more than I say: 'Good for you!', when reading newspaper articles about company responses to significant social and political issues. Many companies have taken the strategic decision to maintain a low profile on reputation risk issues, but claim to be doing a lot of work 'behind the scenes': lobbying politicians, influencing the media, sponsoring research and so on. This is all very well, but in the absence of a strong and confident public position, the perception can be that the company is hiding from the issue. And it leaves the agenda – and the company's reputation – in the hands of others.

The argument that I often hear against being more bold and resolute is that companies 'may win the argument, but can never win the PR battle against governments or interest groups'. The case studies that are usually used to back this argument up are McLibel (in which McDonald's took two environmental campaigners to court for libel and ended up with a global reputation nightmare) and Brent Spar (in which Shell had to change its plans to dispose of a disused floating storage tanker in the North Sea after a heated public battle with Greenpeace).

In fact, the problem with McDonald's' action during the McLibel debacle was not that it was too bold, but that it misjudged its opponents and chose the wrong tactics. When a small anti-McDonald's campaign group called London Greenpeace (not in fact related to the real Greenpeace) persisted with a leafleting campaign about McDonald's' corporate practices, the company finally decided to do something: it threatened to send in the lawyers. But the small campaign group had nothing to lose, and a court case was a godsend in terms of publicity and a perfect set piece to showcase its views and concerns. Whilst the company won the legal battle in the end (and £40,000 in damages, which, unsurprisingly, McDonald's did not pursue), it was a pyrrhic victory in that it had clearly lost in the court of public opinion. The lesson is that being bold and assertive does not mean being headstrong and arrogant. McDonald's has changed since this episode and is far more transparent. This has given it the ability to be more assertive and more confident than ever before.

For Shell, the option of keeping quiet was never on the table. The Brent Spar controversy was sparked by, and subsequently led by, Greenpeace. The issue was about how best to dispose of a disused North Sea floating storage tanker. Shell believed that its preferred disposal method of sinking the spar into the deep ocean was the most environmentally friendly option. Greenpeace disagreed and launched an aggressive media campaign to force what it believed to be a more environmentally sensitive disposal method on the company. When some European governments, under sustained attack by the environmentalists, withdrew their support for Shell's proposals, the oil giant was forced into a radical rethink.

Again, the lesson here is not: 'Don't take on the campaign groups', it is: 'If you're going to take on the campaign groups, choose the right tactics.'

Shell's problem was that it failed to communicate the fact-based assessment that its preferred disposal method was the right one. The company was fighting emotion and visuals with science. This simply does not work. In the battle for hearts and minds, emotion beats science hands down every time. The problem was therefore not that Shell stood up for itself and its plans, but that it did so in a way that failed to engage the ultimate stakeholders: the public. This does not have to mean the 'end of rational argument', but it does mean that rational argument can only win through in the public domain if it is accompanied by emotional appeal, visual imagery and human interest.

The mindset changes I am advocating to senior company executives can be summarized in the following 10 tips:

1. *If you believe it, say it.* And be prepared to stick by it. A company's view is as valid as anyone else's.
2. *Rediscover corporate courage.* Don't shy away from fights on important issues, especially when the agendas of the main players are far apart: if you can't join them, beat them!
3. *Accentuate the positives.* Feel and express no shame about corporate success and achievements. Remember, profit pays for pensions, tax pays for services and corporate success creates jobs and wealth.
4. *Don't accept the blame for global societal issues.* Poverty is not the fault of business; disease is not the fault of business; obesity is not the fault of business; terrorism is not the fault of business. So, don't sit there and tolerate arguments that business is to blame for everything.
5. *Be positive about the future.* The world has always had problems, and always will. But business has led the way before, and it will do so again.
6. *See reputation as a long-term game.* The vicious circle of short-term thinking, which all players in the global game are prone to, must be broken. If you can sacrifice short-term gain to make a long-term reputation difference, be courageous and go for it.
7. *Be a 'reputation realist'.* Accept that some people are against you, and that this is not a bad thing. If you are all things to all people, you are probably being insincere to someone.
8. *Get key issues back on to your territory.* If others control the agenda, you will always be in 'respond and defend' mode.
9. *Don't talk reputation, 'do' reputation.* If the reputation of your company is currently managed by a harassed-looking team of three in corporate relations, get it into the company as a whole. Reputation is nothing unless it is everything.
10. *Be prepared, not arrogant.* However confident and resolute you are, however strong your contribution to key public debates, there are always surprises in business. Never let your guard down, as crises have a habit of striking when you least want them.

Companies have always had potential power, and on many occasions, they have used their power irresponsibly. Companies make mistakes, sometimes for the right reasons and sometimes for the wrong reasons. But companies are not intrinsically bad, as some people seem to want to make out.

The movement that has made the biggest difference to the world in the last 20 years, I would argue, is the anti-capitalist or anti-globalization political movement, which has not only had a deep effect on public opinion, but also corporate communications. The pendulum swung away from business as companies changed their language from: 'We must fight our corner', to: 'We must engage with our stakeholders.' Companies have been on the back foot ever since. But there is evidence that the pendulum might be swinging back again. Hopefully, this time the right balance will be found.

Putting reputation at the heart of the business

The second of the big picture changes is a strategic change, which builds on point nine in the list above: 'don't talk reputation, "do" reputation'.

As suggested in Chapter 1, reputation and reputation management are now well-established corporate buzzwords. One often hears statements like 'reputation is a boardroom issue in our company', and 'we believe that reputation is our greatest asset.' I think reputation is a little bit like Rollerblades and Rubik's Cubes: everybody bought in to the craze, but not many people cracked it. Or, if you prefer, it's the difference between awareness and understanding. Just as everyone is aware of $E = MC^2$ but few understand it, everyone is now aware of 'reputation' but few know really what it means. So, when people say to me that reputation is 'at the heart of our business' and that everyone at their company 'values and wants to protect our reputation', I am rarely convinced.

I recently met through a mutual friend a structured finance executive for a large investment bank. After he explained his job to me (he specializes in putting finance deals together for huge infrastructure projects in parts of Africa), he asked me what I did for a living. I told him that I did 'reputation management'. His face fell. Clearly, his experience of reputation managers had been a bad one. He explained:

Before every project can go ahead, we have to go through a reputation risk assessment process. It is painful, it holds up the process and is completely unnecessary. When you've spent months putting together finance for a project involving multinational companies, local companies, national governments and other lenders, having the whole thing put on ice whilst someone assesses the media interest and the concerns of local environmental groups seems ridiculous.

I told him that I completely agreed with him. After further discussion, it transpired that he had completely bought in to the *concept* of managing reputation, but that he felt entirely divorced from the *process* of it. To him, it was a threat to all his hard work. Thousands of hours and millions of dollars were on the line as the 'reputation inspectors' came round to tell him what he already knew about 'environmental issues really picking up in this part of Africa' and 'media taking a more aggressive line on the power of multinationals'.

I asked him how many times a project had been stopped by this 'reputation check' process. He said that no project that he knew of had ever been stopped. Of course, no project has ever been stopped at this late stage. And that's precisely why reputation should not be treated as a final tick in the box of a massive project. That is not 'reputation management at the heart of business', it is reputation management as an awkward and unpopular add-on.

And yet, we see this all the time. The company I run has often been called into a project that is practically sitting there waiting to have its red ribbon cut and told: 'We think we should just check the reputation impacts before we go ahead.' We are then as popular with the people who have been working on the project as cake hygiene inspectors at a children's birthday party. The role we are asked to play is often, in so many words, to spot any (minor) problems, to make some (minor) suggestions but generally to give the project the reputational all-clear. Of course, it doesn't always work out that way.

Reputation is not the only example of where internal conversations do not happen early enough. Sony recently showed how its marketing department and technical department were seemingly on very different pages in the run up to the launch of its new PlayStation product. Of course, advertising campaigns don't happen overnight, but creating market hype about a forthcoming product that then has technical difficulties is a high-risk strategy. French aircraft-maker

Airbus is currently in reputation and business meltdown thanks to its failure to meet in technical terms what it had promised in emotional terms. What should be its biggest triumph – the Airbus A380 – is, at the time of writing, in danger of becoming its biggest liability.

So, if joined-up thinking is difficult in all aspects of business, how can something as vague as reputation truly be put at the heart of a company? The most important point here is that people respond more to tangible and emotional positives than they do to hypothetical negatives. Reputation must be seen as something worth having and building, not just something that it is catastrophic to lose. Perhaps, for the structured finance project manager, the reputation management selling words are something like:

> Would you agree that it would be good for the long-term success of the project if, when it gets off the ground, there is broad support for it from local communities and the media? Wouldn't it be good if internally this can be seen as a best practice project because it became so popular? To help you make this happen, can we help you in the early stages of this project rather than just at the end?

Ultimately, the solution is about an internal sales job and increased understanding. It is about a much wider internal audience understanding $E = MC^2$ as well as having heard of it. It is about being taught how to skate on rollerblades rather than just having a pair sitting on your desk when you arrive at work one morning with a note saying 'these are great, so don't lose them'.

Training, reward, ownership, empowerment... there are many ways to try to get reputation genuinely to the heart of the organization. It has to start from the top, but it must not get stalled in the communications department. And it must be action-based, not word-based.

One challenge I think works well: take a group of employees from any level or any function and ask them to brainstorm initiatives to enhance or protect the organization's reputation. Then, ask them to eliminate any that are about communicating lofty commitments and values or investing in good causes. See what you have left. If you have next to nothing left, then your organization talks the talk on reputation, but it doesn't really understand it. If you have some good action-based ideas left, escalate them to someone who has the power to take them further.

Redrawing the corporate stakeholder map and engagement plan

The third change in this section may seem like a fairly mundane tactical change, but is in fact a crucial change to the corporate mind-set on reputation management: redrawing the stakeholder map.

If stakeholder engagement is corporate speak for 'talking and listening to people who matter to us and our business', then it makes sense to categorize these people and map them out in some way to understand how they are all interrelated. But, as was suggested by the workshop story in the introduction to this book, what comes out of this exercise is often a flawed model for truly understanding and dealing with the organization's audiences.

At a recent PR conference, Philip Dewhurst, then head of communications for British Nuclear Fuels Limited, said that a stakeholder is 'anyone who has the potential to bugger up your business'.[8] I agree, but the next step in this train of thought is often wrong because, at the head of the stakeholder list, you will almost always find governments and campaign groups. They, after all, are the most visible and dangerous potential opponents. The campaign groups will be under the banner 'NGO', which itself might be subcategorized into headings covering the Environment, Industrial Relations, Human Rights and so on. Also on the stakeholder list will be a 'Media' category – local, regional, national. There will be a section called 'Employment', which has, amongst others, the subcategories of 'Trade Unions', 'Head Office Staff' and 'Other'.

There may not seem much wrong with this, but there is something subtly very wrong with it. There is no purpose, direction and emphasis; it is just a list. Even if it is a prioritized list, it is essentially a list of organizations that are easily listable. That's why Friends of the Earth is on it (website, contact details, easy to send reports to), but a genuine local community that has different and more real concerns about the environment (not organized, passive, expensive to send reports to) is probably not. The most important stakeholders are probably the consumers who buy your products and are broadly supportive but sometimes have concerns about your company. But they do not have a website, an address and a spokesperson who can easily be 'engaged with'. What stakeholder lists often end up being, therefore, are lists of opinion formers. This might be a useful list, but it is not really a stakeholder list. This might sound pedantic, but there is a very real danger that these opinion former lists are seen by companies as an acceptable substitute for talking to and listening to the real stakeholders.

With this in mind, what follows in the box below is a new way of thinking about and ordering stakeholders, which might help organizations to establish a new mindset.

Company X's stakeholder list

We at Company X have many stakeholders and we want to engage with as many of them as possible. We must prioritize, of course, but that does not mean going to those that are easily identifiable. Our priorities are as follows:

Priority 1   The people without whose active support we can't operate:
Customers, who buy our products and services
Employees, who make and sell our products and services
Shareholders, who finance the company
Local communities, who support our continued operations where they live

Priority 2   The people who hold power over us:
Governments, who can withdraw our licence to operate
Regulators, who can report perceived or real failings and can withdraw our licence to operate

Priority 3   People who influence those in the above categories:
The media, who have some control over our public image
Interest groups, who also talk to key audiences
Experts, who can have an influence in their field over the above audiences

Priority 4   People who want to see us fail:
Campaign groups, who oppose what we do and what we stand for
Competitors, who have no interest in seeing us succeed (although they might not always want us to fail, lest we take the whole industry's reputation down)

A central argument in this book is that many companies are engaging with the wrong groups on the wrong agenda and the wrong issues. Recasting the stakeholder list and map will not solve this problem, but it is a tangible shift towards getting the reputation priorities right.

Summary

At the beginning of this chapter, I quoted from Cadbury Schweppes Chief Executive Todd Stitzer. His *Financial Times* article in summer 2006 was an interesting and important contribution to the debate about corporate image and reputation management, in which he appeared to be advocating a more confident and combative strategy. But just a matter of weeks after the article appeared, Cadbury Schweppes saw its own reputation severely threatened after a large-scale product recall in the United Kingdom sparked by a salmonella scare. The company emerged from the crisis with its business intact, but its reputation badly scarred. I have not heard Mr Stitzer giving any more advice on reputation to his corporate peers.

Being bold on the big issues, standing up for business and 'regaining the reputation initiative' is not something that can be done in isolation from good day-to-day management of issues and crises. It is hard to take a public stand on something when the perception is that your own house is not in order.

Changing the corporate mindset, getting reputation genuinely to the heart of the organization and redrawing the stakeholder engagement list are just the start to regaining the reputation initiative. To make a real difference, the same thinking needs to be applied to the various aspects of managing reputation risk. The rest of this book looks at the three key areas of reputation risk management – crisis management, issues management and CSR – and makes recommendations for change in each.

Notes

1. Stitzer, T (1 June 2006) *Financial Times*, 'Business Must Loudly Proclaim What It Stands For'.
2. Reuters (14 February 2007) 'TOTAL's Record Profits Stir Up French Election'.

3. *Financial Times* (14 February 2007) 'Business Leaders Warn Against Royal Victory'.
4. *The Guardian* (5 January 2007) 'Labour Targets Airlines Over Carbon Emissions'.
5. *The Independent* (6 January 2007) 'Government Should Look to Mote in its Own Eye Before Branding O'Leary Irresponsible'.
6. *The Times* (25 April 2007) 'Most Britons Believe that Airlines are Failing to Clear the Air'.
7. *Financial Times* (6 March 2007).
8. Philip Dewhurst quoted in *PRWeek* (11 December 2006).

4 Crisis management – leadership in a tried and tested system

If you have read what has gone before in this book, you will be forgiven for thinking that crisis management is becoming less important than management of the big societal issues and corporate reputation as a whole. It is not. Yes, good crisis preparedness is only one part of managing the ever-multiplying risks to reputation presented by the increasingly hostile outside world, but it is more important than ever.

If you have not read what has gone before, I doubt you are alone. More than a few people will, I suspect, flick straight to this chapter because crisis management – or crisis communications in particular – is regarded as one of the most interesting parts of corporate communications. Reading the latest case studies of crisis management is the PR equivalent of 'car crash TV' – we all love to see other people making an absolute hopeless mess of a difficult situation. This is one reason why crisis management remains absolutely vital in protecting reputation: we all love to wallow in a good crisis, and the media are more than well aware of that. That is why even a relatively minor coach crash involving a party of children will routinely knock war, collapsing stock markets, global warming, famine, pandemic disease and almost everything else off the top of the news agenda.

This chapter looks at what the changing external environment means for crisis management and makes various recommendations for companies wanting to prepare themselves for the worst. It places increased emphasis on leadership and competence – complementing rather than replacing procedures and systems – as the core differentiators in crisis management.

First, some clarity of definition is needed. For the purposes of this chapter, and to differentiate crises from issues, I will define a crisis as an 'acute' risk to reputation: a crisis happens suddenly, leads to intense scrutiny and puts your organization in the spotlight for all the wrong reasons.

Crisis management – easy in theory

Crises are the most public of all the collisions on the corporate collision course. But, in theory they are the easiest to manage because they are all about implementing something that has been prepared in advance. That is what companies do well. Ask a food company whether it feels more confident managing a consumer recall or defending its products in the obesity debate, and most will feel they have the former covered. That is because the former has a manual and can be rehearsed; the latter is ever evolving and unpredictable. Oil companies will probably tell you the same: an oil spill is manageable; global warming and local community objections to a refinery are tricky.

A crisis should be about pushing the button on a well-honed response. Everyone knows where to go, what to do, what their responsibilities are and what the organization expects of them. There are dedicated crisis rooms, crisis phones, crisis procedures, crisis toolkits, crisis phone lists and crisis management agencies. If everything slots in to place just like it did when the crisis exercise was held a few months back, it should all be fine.

It never quite works like that.

But, even if it doesn't go like clockwork from the beginning, there is another reason why crisis management should be easier than managing other reputation risks: the public is on your side. For the crucial first few hours of a crisis involving actual or potential loss of life or injury, the prevailing public climate is a benign one. Let me explain this with a fairly obvious example: a plane crash.

If you were to turn on your television this evening and see that there had been a plane crash in your state or region, you would almost certainly be interested. If the recovery operation was developing in front of your eyes, you would be unlikely to switch channels. A tragedy of this nature is the ultimate human-interest story.

The first feeling you would have is shock. After the initial shock and once you had taken in the basics of what has happened, you would probably start to personalize the crisis. You would think through how you might be affected (you might worry about certain people you knew were flying on that day) and then once you are confident that you are not affected you would work out how you *could* potentially have been affected: 'I have flown with them so many times before'; 'my husband used to travel on that route'; 'I think my sister-in-law used to work for that airline' and so on.

As you watch the crisis unfold, you would start to feel a sense of empathy for the people involved: the injured, the relatives of the dead arriving at the airport, the emergency services battling to save human life. You would be hoping for the best and wanting everyone to come through the crisis. What you would probably not feel at this early stage is any sense of anger towards the airline. You would (hopefully) see airline representatives briefing the media and you would not feel that they were evil corporate killers. Even if there is reason to believe that the crash was caused by human or mechanical error (ie, the airline seems to have been at fault), you are still too caught up in the human emotion of the tragedy to start apportioning blame. Furthermore, were the media to be giving the airline representative a serious grilling about safety when bodies were still being taken from the burning wreck, you would think this inappropriate. The media know this, which is why they don't do it. Blame comes later.

So, at the beginning of any major physical crisis, the public is almost always rooting for the company involved, whatever its reputation. Whatever you think of a specific airline, you would want it to respond well to a crisis that saw 100 of its customers and 10 of its staff killed. Whilst at a later date you might mentally use the crisis to reinforce your opinion that this airline is a bad company, in the heat of the crisis you are at least temporarily on its side.

If this seems unlikely (perhaps there are companies you hate so much that you can't imagine ever wanting them to get something right), think about it on a smaller scale. For example, you may hate your neighbour but, if his or her house caught fire, you would probably not rejoice or think that it serves them right. Indeed, we want heroes in crises, and unlikely heroes are the best of all. Your neighbour may be a criminal who has just returned from jail but, if he rescues his family from a burning building, he will be a hero for the day. The media coverage will be all about how a crisis brings out the best in people and how human goodness can triumph over character failings.

So, not only is crisis preparedness a fairly straightforward stepwise process – write the crisis manual, train people to use it, test them with regular scenario exercises – but actual crisis management is often managed in a context of (albeit temporary) support and/or sympathy.

Why, then, are there still so many examples of poor crisis management? Why do I have such a long list of recent crises to choose from as case study material? The answer is that crisis management is far less easy in practice than it is in theory, and the window of public support for the organization at the heart of the crisis is often short-lived.

Furthermore, however well-prepared you are as a company, however comprehensive the crisis procedures, however well-rehearsed the crisis management team, there is nothing quite as stressful and draining as a major crisis. To have the world's media at your door hour after hour, day after day, is stressful; to have employees or customers at risk because of something that has happened to your company is stressful; to have the future of your company in your hands as you head off to meet the press, the shareholders or the regulators is stressful. No crisis manual can take away the stress and emotion that crisis responsibilities create; no public support in the early hours can mitigate those feelings. Crises may seem more systematically manageable than other reputation risks, but there is absolutely no room for complacency.

This chapter is not a 'how to' guide for crisis management. My colleague Mike Regester – the undisputed guru of crisis management – has written extensively on this.[1] Some of the basics will be covered as and when appropriate, but the chapter looks to improve best practice rather than reprise it. The five key points that this chapter will focus on are:

1.   Crisis management is about substance, not spin.
2.   You're not alone.
3.   Prepare your people as well as your process.
4.   Practice makes perfect.
5.   Leadership is the key differentiator.

Crisis management is about substance, not spin

When I introduce myself to people as a crisis communications consultant, one of the most popular responses is: 'Ah, so when something goes wrong, you're the one that covers it up/tells us it's not all that bad.' I think this is possibly how the Iraqi Information Minister Mohammed Saeed al-Sahhaf (also known as Comical Ali) saw his job during the early days of war in Iraq – you may remember he became known for such utterances as: 'Now even the American command is under siege. We are hitting it from the north, east, south and west. We are the people laying siege to them. And it is not them who are besieging us.' But this is not how I see my job. The truth is you cannot spin your way out of a crisis. This can cause some confusion within companies, with some senior executives still thinking that the process of making the decisions and communicating with the outside world are two entirely separate things. But, thankfully, the mentality of 'we'll manage the crisis, you manage the media' is slowly disappearing, at least in multinationals.

The best crisis responses in my experience are those in which the head of communications and his/her team are as integral to decision-making as the operations people and business continuity people. This comes back to one of the key themes of the book: it is impossible to compartmentalize reputation. To some operational people, this is hard to stomach. They often believe that there is a scientific or technical 'right thing to do' and that image or reputation benefits will flow from doing the right thing in a crisis. But the right thing to do has to be driven by emotional rather than technical factors.

For example, if an oil spill results in oil washing up onto a beach, it might be the right operational decision to let the whole slick wash up before starting to clean the beach, but it is the wrong emotional decision. People need to see action, and having a team of company volunteers cleaning the beach is visually powerful, even if the beach is blackened again the next time the tide comes in. Good communications professionals will insist that the emotional overrides the technical in a case like this.

Another more complicated example would be with a food scare. If you are the crisis management team of a dairy company, and you have been convened because tests have identified a possible contamination of your milk products, which are already in the market, when is the right time to communicate with consumers? If you are being advised that the worst case scenario is 1 per cent of consumers getting minor food poisoning, do you wait until all tests are complete to identify where these customers might be? This risks people drinking the product and falling ill when you could have stopped it. Or do you issue a total consumer recall immediately, risking a health panic and possible strain on health services, as you know that much of the product will already have been consumed? As with this example, the right thing to do is not always evident, and is based on emotion and sense as much as science. Again, the communications professional must advise the crisis team on how the emotional aspects of the various options will play amongst consumers and the media, and how the decisions will be perceived after the event.

Another popular misconception is that crisis communication is about communicating soothing words in a difficult situation. To a certain extent, it is: when something dreadful happens, we want to see and hear company representatives telling us how they feel about what has happened, and what they are doing to make the situation better. People, however, are not stupid and they will not tolerate platitudes for long. Take the example of a factory explosion in which dozens of employees are injured. The factory manager or senior corporate representative will probably be media-trained to say things like: 'Safety is our number one priority and we are committed to doing whatever we can to help those colleagues who have been affected by this terrible incident.' This is fine for the first hour or so. Thereafter, people want to see action and hear details. What exactly are you doing to help the affected people? What gives you the right to claim that safety is your number one priority? What are you going to do to ensure this never happens again? If you do not have the answers to these questions, the crisis response is inadequate. Crisis communications is about communicating actions, not just picking the right words.

One of the fundamental principles of crisis management that you will hear from crisis communications specialists is: 'If you're doing the right thing, make sure the world knows about it.' There is no point in getting the operational response right if the public perceives that you are not doing it. Again, this can be uncomfortable for senior operational managers or the top decision-makers. On many occasions, crisis specialists will find themselves trying to persuade the chief executive of a company going through a crisis to take a few hours out of the crisis management team to conduct media interviews. The response is sometimes: 'My job is here, to steer the company through the crisis. If we get it right, the media will see the result and our reputation will be saved.' This is well-intentioned and logical, but wrong. The order of priorities in a crisis is not: 'Do it, then explain it', it is: 'Explain it as you are doing it.'

Another element of this is the selection of the most appropriate company spokesperson. This is not always the chief executive (you don't want to escalate unnecessarily if the crisis is not a major one) but if the situation calls for senior spokespeople, they must be persuaded to take the uncomfortable step from operational control to media management.

An example of communication initially succeeding but then failing to protect reputation as the substance proved inadequate is BP's 'fall from grace' since the explosion and fire at the company's Texas City Refinery on 23 March 2005, in which 15 people were killed. Up until this point, BP enjoyed an enviable reputation. It was run by one of the corporate world's most admired leaders, Lord Browne, it had outflanked its rivals on perceptions of environmental responsibility and it had largely avoided the attention that Shell and Exxon had received for corporate responsibility issues. This reputation has now nosedived.

But the fall from grace did not happen overnight. In fact, the company's immediate response to the Texas City Refinery disaster was seemingly in line with its reputation: it was seen to be doing and heard to be saying all the right things. Indeed, I remember making a speech shortly thereafter, in which I said that the company had made a huge withdrawal from its high credit in the reputation bank, but that the response to Texas City was a good example of crisis communication.

Whilst this initial crisis response staved off immediate reputation damage, the subsequent enquiries exposed organizational failings within the company. Furthermore, additional crises and issues added to the damage. Soon, BP's brand was tarnished and the media were on the lookout for further banana skins.

The conclusion is that, in the climate of high scrutiny and low trust, the truth comes out in the end. People will forgive errors, and they will forgive crises if they are handled well, but they will not so easily forgive companies that do not appear to have done everything they could have done to avoid crises happening in the first place. Good crisis communication can buy time, but it cannot alone save reputation. This is why reputation has to be something that is understood, felt and managed through the entire company. BP's fall from grace is more fully described in the case study below.

Reputation reversed – BP's fall from grace

BP's reputation woes began on Wednesday 23 March 2005. At the Texas City Refinery – the second largest oil refinery in Texas, processing around 450,000 barrels of crude oil per day – a cloud of volatile hydrocarbon vapour ignited after it had escaped from an octane unit. Fifteen people were killed and 170 injured.

BP's crisis communications efforts seemed to be in line with best practice: this is a high-profile oil major that rehearses its people for just such terrible scenarios. The most senior people in the organization were seen to be taking the right actions and heard to be expressing the right sentiments. Lord Browne visited the scene, saying it was the worst tragedy he had known during his 38 years with the company: 'All of us have been profoundly affected. All of us want to know what happened... I came to Texas City to assure people the full resources of BP will be there to help the bereaved and the injured... I spent the morning with the men and women that operate and maintain the refinery. I have heard many harrowing stories but the team is in very strong spirits.'

Lord Browne also promised that BP's 'best people' would be deployed immediately to investigate the cause of the explosion and said the company would 'cooperate fully with government officials responsible for examining the circumstances of this terrible explosion and fire'. Asked if the explosion was an accident waiting to happen, Lord Browne said: 'I don't believe it was. There is no stone left unturned in making sure all events are investigated and remediation is done after the event. There is no limit to the amount of action we have undertaken. It is a very safe plant. If there is more to be done we will do it.'

The day after the Texas City Refinery explosion, the media seemed to be giving BP a fair hearing and the coverage was fairly benign. The *Wall Street Journal* gave credit for Lord Browne's actions: 'In a sign of how seriously the company was taking the incident, Lord Browne flew to Texas City yesterday and pledged to "leave nothing undone in our effort to determine the cause of the tragedy".'[2]

The *Financial Times* said that BP 'will need more than sympathetic words and free meals for the families hit by the blast to repair its tarnished reputation'. Indeed. But the newspaper was also complimentary of Lord Browne: 'In moving swiftly, Lord Browne has avoided the negative fall-out that hit ExxonMobil when its tanker ran aground in Alaska, creating the largest oil spill in the US. Many bristled at the perceived arrogant tone of ExxonMobil, whose chairperson left subordinates to deal with the crisis. In contrast, Lord Browne has been suitably humble.'[3]

The crisis response had worked well, and the company's reputation had remained intact in these early stages. But this was not to last. It soon became apparent that the refinery had a chequered safety record leading up to the explosion. In March 2004, the refinery had been evacuated after an explosion, costing the company US$63,000 in fines. In September 2004, two workers had died and one was injured when they were scalded by superheated water that had escaped from a high pressure pipe.

BP's own interim report into the March 2005 blast, completed by mid-May, concluded that managers had failed to supervise the isomerization unit, operators were absent at crucial periods and that they failed to take corrective action early enough. It also said that the refinery's working environment 'had eroded to one characterized by resistance to change, and lacking of trust, motivation and a sense of purpose'. It was BP's stated intention to offer 'fair compensation' to the families of the deceased and injured without the need for litigation. Initially, BP allocated US$700 million to compensate the victims of the explosion. This was raised to US$1.2 billion in July 2006. In September 2006, BP settled its final lawsuit just before a jury was to be sworn in for what would have been the first civil case resulting from the explosion.

In December 2005, the US Department of Labor referred the Texas City case to the Department of Justice, raising the possibility of BP facing criminal charges in the United States. The referral came after a US Occupational Safety and Health Administration investigation, which found more than 300 violations of health and safety standards at the refinery. During this month, BP announced that it would spend US$1 billion on the Texas City Refinery over the following five years.

The Baker Panel report, led by former US Secretary of State James A Baker, was released in January 2007 and found 'material deficiencies' in BP's safety procedures at its US oil refineries. The report said that BP emphasized personal safety but not process safety, and that the problem existed at all five of the firm's refineries in the United States. It said: 'BP mistakenly interpreted improving personal injury rates as an indication of acceptable process safety performance at its US refineries. The panel found instances of a lack of operating discipline, toleration of serious deviations from safe operating practices, and apparent complacency toward serious safety risks at each refinery.'

By this time, the media had turned against BP. The initial crisis response was forgotten, and coverage was now about a company that had not implemented safety policies properly over a period of years. The headlines were now about how there had been warning signs for several years, how cost-cutting was to blame and how the company must now repair its tarnished reputation.[4]

But reputation repair was made more difficult by other crises. On 2 March 2006, a worker for BP Exploration (Alaska) discovered a large oil spill at Prudhoe Bay. At least 6,350 barrels had spilled (more than 250,000 gallons of crude oil), making it the largest spill to date in Alaska's North Slope region. In September, congressmen and women accused BP of 'unacceptable' neglect of pipelines in Alaska at a congressional hearing.

And then came the price manipulation allegations. Regulators claimed that BP Products North America artificially forced up prices of propane in 2004 by buying huge stocks and then withholding them from the market. The Commodities Futures Trading Commission (CFTC) alleged that manipulation was carried out 'with the knowledge, advice and consent of senior management'. BP claimed that price manipulation did not occur.

The year 2006 was truly an 'annus horribilis' for BP. The company had been transformed from one with an enviable reputation to one that was regularly pilloried by the media. It started the previous year with a good crisis management response, which may have helped keep civil claims to a manageable level, but this was soon forgotten as more details emerged and as other reputation incidents occurred. Furthermore, BP's reputation as a leader in the environmental debate suffered. As *The Independent* newspaper in the United Kingdom said, 'so much for the "Beyond Petroleum" slogans launched by the eco-friendly behemoth'.[5]

Businessman and investor Warren Buffet once said that 'it takes 20 years to build a reputation and five minutes to ruin it'. BP's reputation was not destroyed in five minutes or in the instant aftermath of the Texas City Refinery blast. It was destroyed over time, as the correct actions and sentiments made and uttered on the day of the blast were exposed as spin not substance. Further events and allegations added weight to the media's u-turn on the company that once seemed to be almost unanimously admired.

You're not alone

This may seem like a blindingly obvious point, but it is an important one: crisis management does not happen in a vacuum. If an incident or escalation is significant enough for your organization to declare it a crisis, there is a high likelihood that other organizations will do the same. And yet only a very small proportion of the crisis exercises that take place involve more than one organization.

An examination of the anatomy of a major physical crisis in the case study below – the Buncefield oil storage facility crisis from December 2005 – demonstrates this point.

Buncefield – whose crisis is it anyway?

On Sunday 11 December 2005, an explosion at the Buncefield oil depot – run by Hertfordshire Oil Storage Limited (HOSL), a joint venture between TOTAL and Chevron – woke people up to 50 miles away (it measured 2.4 on the Richter scale). The smoke from what became the biggest fire in peacetime Europe shrouded the sky in the south of England. Fortunately, no one died and only two people needed hospital treatment.

The disruption caused to the surrounding area by the explosion was immense: 80 companies, employing 4,000 people, were left without premises; there was structural damage to over 300 homes with 2,000 residents evacuated; approximately 200 Hertfordshire and Buckinghamshire schools were closed for two days; two of the main motorways in the United Kingdom were closed for a time; and there was fuel rationing at Heathrow Airport (the depot supplied Heathrow via a pipeline). In total, 3,300 claims, worth a potential £700 million, have been filed by residents, businesses and insurers.

The following is a list of ten – by no means all – of the organizations that were in crisis management mode after the explosion and fire:

1. *HOSL (TOTAL UK/Chevron)* The oil companies' crisis teams acted quickly to provide support to the emergency services and the local community. They set up assistance helplines, a repair and assistance team to help with immediate emergency property repairs and a confidential counselling service. They donated £150,000 to the Mayors' Recovery Fund as well as additional financial donations to the Salvation Army and the Red Cross.

2. *UKPIA* The UK Petroleum Industry Association convened its crisis team to manage the knock-on effects of the explosion on the UK oil supply, bringing all other major oil companies into the loop. UKPIA also led the industry's media response. The organization significantly took the heat off the oil companies by being available to supply information about safety and operational regulations at UK facilities.

3. *The emergency services* The emergency services led the immediate operational response, making the important operational decisions, such as the best way to extinguish the fire, which roads to close and so on. Hertfordshire Constabulary did not have the capacity to meet the needs of the incident and so called in the help of forces from around the United Kingdom. The media were understandably keen to find heroes from the emergency services, and to get comment from those closest to the blaze. The police and fire rescue services were thus often commenting in the media about the incident.

4. *Environment Agency* The environmental regulator was present at the scene very quickly, eager to begin its investigation. In 1996, the Environment Agency (for England and Wales) took over the roles and responsibilities of other bodies: the National Rivers Authority, Her Majesty's Inspectorate of Pollution (HMIP) and the waste regulation authorities in England and Wales.

5. *Health and Safety Executive* The HSE was also key as the crisis unfolded. As the catch-all government body for health and safety, the HSE reports to the Health and Safety Commission and is therefore under pressure to be efficient, especially with an incident the size of Buncefield.

6. *Heathrow Airport and the British Airports Authority* The Buncefield complex acted as a main pipeline transit point to meet 40 per cent of Heathrow Airport's demand for aviation fuel. The explosions resulted in a shortage, and BAA thus needed a crisis response of its own.

7. *The office of Mike Penning MP* Hemel Hempstead is a parliamentary constituency represented by Conservative MP Mike Penning. After the incident, he positioned himself as the 'voice of the people', which was helped by his status as a former firefighter.

8. *The Office of the Deputy Prime Minister* The Deputy Prime Minister, John Prescott, and his team were heavily involved in the crisis response. The ODPM acts as the central government department for major crises that are not squarely in the territory of any of the other departments of state. Mr Prescott visited the site a few days after the explosion and was high on the stakeholder list of all other organizations.

9. *Dacorum Borough Council* The local council provided updates on its website, released press statements and held press conferences.

10. *Local businesses* With 80 companies left without premises, it is likely that dozens of crisis plans were implemented within the business community. A key role was played by the Hertfordshire Chamber of Commerce, which set up helplines for businesses, offering help and advice about insurance companies and solicitors.

In a major crisis, it is quite possible that hundreds of individuals representing dozens of organizations will be involved. One organization may be perceived as being at the centre of the crisis response, but others will not stand aside and allow that organization to dominate. Remember, reputations are on the line for all organizations; all need to be seen to be doing the right things and all need to be heard to be saying the right things. This means that dozens of crisis procedures may be invoked in any major incident. Do they all dovetail nicely together? Do all participants understand each other's roles and requirements? Of course not. There will never be a major crisis in which all of the organizations involved know each other's procedures and people in great depth, but this does not mean that it should be 'every organization for itself'.

A good discipline is to invite at least two stakeholders to participate in every major crisis exercise, either as role players or observers. This builds understanding of procedures and culture and also builds relationships between people who may have to work closely together in a real crisis. Whether you are preparing behaviours or processes for crisis management, it is always wise to remember: in a crisis, you are not alone.

Prepare your people as well as your process

Many companies still place far too great an emphasis on process over people. The reality is that processes are necessary, but they don't manage crises. People manage crises.

This over-reliance on 'the manual' is something that has come from what Professor Mitroff calls the 'hostile takeover' of crisis management by business continuity planning.[6] The people who put together the business continuity plans tend to be technical experts or engineers. They tend to be problem-solvers, and have an eye for detail that few communications professionals, salespeople, HR managers or brand specialists can even imagine. This is fine, because these latter professionals should not be involved with the logistics of the business continuity plan. But, if the crisis management manual is either part of, or in the same style as, the business continuity plan, a difficulty emerges.

To understand the effect of this, we need to step back and define exactly what crisis management is about. I would suggest that good crisis management comprises strong leadership within a defined and well-understood organizational structure that is peopled by competent and trained professionals implementing rehearsed processes. There are four elements there, two of which – leadership and competence – are behavioural and two of which – structure and process – are systemic. Both are important, but if I had to choose between a crisis response that had good systems but poor skills and one that had good skills but poor systems, I would go for the good skills every time.

In my experience, this is not the way most companies order things. For many companies, systems rule. Manuals are tangible. But just as the military will tell you that no military engagement plan survives first contact with the enemy, no crisis manual survives the first hours of a crisis. So something else is needed. If you ask the people who have to manage crises whether they want more tools or more training, the answer is normally clear: 'We want training.' Training boosts confidence.

Towards the end of one crisis exercise that I ran for a travel company, my client turned to me and pointed at the neatly bound crisis manuals sitting redundant on a side table. 'No one has even looked at them once', she said despondently, 'they should all have them open in front of them. I don't know why we bothered.' I said that it depended on why they were not opening the manuals. If the participants are not opening them because they already know the contents and their responsibilities, that would be a good sign (after all, if I was in an aircraft that was faltering, I'd want the pilot to know what to do rather than have to look it up in his or her manual). If, however, they are not opening the crisis manual because they do not understand it, they do not see the value of it or they do not know it exists, then that is something to worry about.

There is another problem with an over-reliance on process documents. It is actually very difficult to read anything in a crisis. It is like trying to eat on a roller coaster. And, with the new external reality of instant and extensive scrutiny, the roller coaster is already moving before you have had time to get the manual out of your briefcase.

There is a time and a place for certain things, and reading complex documents with flow charts is not best done when the media is gathered outside and the chief executive is demanding an update on your actions in 10 minutes. Some people are better at this than others, but generally the atmosphere in a crisis is not conducive to taking in and assimilating important information. It is much better for the crisis team to have a good sense of what the system demands of them, and to use their competence and confidence to make the right choices and take the right actions.

I am absolutely not advocating an end to crisis procedures. The pro-gun lobby in the United States is fond of saying that 'guns don't kill people; people kill people'. Well, yes, but guns certainly help. In the same way, crisis manuals don't manage crises, people do, but the manuals certainly help. Writing manuals, discussing them, explaining them, arguing over them and refreshing them all instil the processes and structures into the minds of those who need to know them. And good procedures can provide a helpful context for training, so the two elements of process and competence can be mutually reinforcing.

Procedures are still crucial, which is why the fact that they are changing is a good sign. They are getting shorter, more user-friendly and less comprehensive. Some companies have binned the A4 bound manuals in favour of a thin A5 folder and a credit-card-sized version that contains the basics. And enlightened companies are realizing that manuals will never provide the answers to the many questions that a crisis poses. They are therefore designing them as enablers, not straitjackets; guidance, not instructions.

After the London bombings of 7 July 2005, a Review Committee was set up to see what lessons could be learned from the crisis response. One of its observations was that 'procedures tend to focus too much on incidents, rather than on individuals, and on processes rather than people'. One of its recommendations was therefore 'a change in mindset... from incidents to individuals, and from processes to people'.[7] I quite agree. The lessons of this crisis, and of all crises, are clear: people must come first. Competent, trained people will find their way through convoluted processes; incompetent, untrained people will make a mess of the best processes in the world. But – best of all – good process can enable competent people to make better judgements.

Practice makes perfect

There is no better way to prepare for a crisis than to practise. Working through a realistic scenario under pressure is an invaluable way to assess the strengths and weaknesses within the crisis response, the abilities of the individuals on the crisis management team(s) and dynamics within and between these teams. Of course, the 'real thing' will pan out differently from the crisis exercise, but that doesn't matter: just because the Brazil national football team's warm-up games against Azerbaijan are a bit different from the World Cup Final against Germany, it doesn't make the practice games irrelevant. Teamwork and skills can and should be learned and practised.

Again, the Buncefield crisis from December 2005 provides a lesson, this time in the value of preparation. At the time of writing, the final report of the Buncefield Major Incident Investigation Board has yet to be published, but the crisis itself was well managed by the oil companies involved and, thanks to good work done by the UK Petroleum Industry Association, by the industry as a whole.

The interesting fact for this section is that the oil companies involved had regularly rehearsed. The crisis proper was therefore run by teams that had practised together and that had been trained over many years to deal with such an eventuality. Many of my colleagues were involved both with the exercises and the real incident. As the crisis unfolded, there was a feeling of preparedness as everything fell into place just as had been rehearsed. Of course, there were unique circumstances and unique challenges, but the response teams were competent and confident, and knew the roles they needed to play.

Exercises do not need to be surprises. In large organizations, exercises require so much preparation and diaries are so difficult to juggle that it is almost impossible to run a meaningful surprise exercise. Some people think that this should be part of the challenge: you don't know when a real crisis is going to happen, so you shouldn't know when the exercise will happen. If the chief executive is out of the country, so be it – the organization needs to learn how to cope without him or her.

But I think knowing the crisis exercise is going to happen actually puts a helpful focus on crisis management skills. If participants are told that they will be part of a crisis exercise in, say, three months time, they will prepare themselves. Nobody wants to put in a poor performance in front of their peers and superiors, so participants may well use the three months to ensure they have the right training and have read the right documents. So if they prepare themselves to 'get it right' in an impending exercise, they are more likely to get it right if a real crisis were to occur. Getting it right is not cheating; getting it right is good!

One final point in this section is that, after a crisis exercise, the lessons learned must be taken on board. There is no merit in an exercise after which, regardless of performance, there is mutual back-slapping. There is also no merit in deconstructing all the mistakes and leaving the participants feeling that the whole exercise exposed their personal weaknesses. A good exercise will leave participants feeling that they did a good job given the structure, systems and leaders they had to work with, but that there is always room for improvement. It should reinforce the culture of crisis-readiness and lead to behavioural changes if necessary. Practice should not engender complacency; it should lead to continuous improvement.

Those who have planned a major international crisis exercise know that it is often a frustrating and always a time-consuming task. It can take at least three months to prepare for a three-hour exercise. It is not always easy to convince senior management of the need for crisis exercises – few like to give up a whole day to be tested in front of their colleagues on something that most find uncomfortable and stressful. But it is most certainly worth it. In crisis management, people matter. And the best way to prepare people is to give them plenty of opportunities to practise.

Leadership is the key differentiator

I cannot overstate the value of good crisis leadership. Suffice it to say, when my colleagues and/or I walk into a crisis room either for the purposes of an exercise or in a real crisis situation, it is apparent within about five minutes whether or not the crisis will be well managed. It just takes a few minutes of observing how the crisis leader consults the team, listens to options, divides up responsibilities, chairs discussions and takes decisions to know where the crisis response is going. So much so, that we see it as a vital part of our role to advise clients if the team leader is floundering.

Renowned leadership guru John Kotter has written that leadership defines a vision of what the future should look like, aligns people with that vision, and inspires them to make it happen despite the obstacles.[8] This is true of leadership at any time, and certainly true of crisis leadership. A good leader must know what he or she wants the end of the crisis to look like and must be able to persuade the team that it is worth achieving and that it can be achieved despite what may seem at the beginning to be a dire situation. In a major crisis, some people round the crisis table will be thinking: 'When this is over, will I have a job?' To get the best from people whose whole world may have been shaken is a tough challenge to say the least.

There is a vast amount of literature on leadership out there, and I do not intend to stray into this field too much. Leadership comes in all shapes and sizes, and there is no one leadership style that is better than another. It is not always the loudest, the most self-confident people who make the best leaders. Nor is it necessarily those who are the nicest people or the most consensual decision-makers. The classic question in assessing an individual's leadership capabilities is: 'Would I follow this person into battle?' In the box below is a list of different types of leadership styles. You may recognize some of them, and although the personal pronoun 'he' has been used here, of course they may be male or female.

Would you follow them into battle?

The patriarch   This leader presides over a company that cannot function – or is not allowed to function – without him (it usually is a 'him'). The culture of the company is not to prepare too much for crises because 'when it happens, he'll run the show his way'. Patriarchs are often unjustifiably confident in their abilities to run a crisis response in the modern world and believe that, were they to be abroad at the time of a crisis, the whole company would fall down. The truth is probably that, given half a chance, his colleagues would run a much better crisis response than he would.

The egomaniac   Unable to listen to advice and unwilling to show weakness, this leader thinks that he is bold and inspiring, but in fact is seen as arrogant. Yes, he can chair a meeting effectively and deal with conflict, but the fact that he is always right (or thinks he is right) is just annoying to others, who will soon be whispering disapprovingly behind his back. The battle cry may be loud and confident, but colleagues may be taking up the sword to stab him in the back rather than to follow him into battle.

The barrister This leader only has ears for one of his crisis team members: the legal counsel. Although he has never been a lawyer himself, the conversation around the crisis table is all about liability, privilege and claims. Whilst for good leaders the lawyer is one of many advisers round the table, for this leader, the lawyer is chief adviser. When he asks: 'What do the lawyers think?', he is not asking for an opinion, but a decision. Other members of the crisis response become demotivated and less effective. The result of this leadership style can be that the company's case is lost in the court of public opinion before it ever makes it to the courts.

The trainspotter This leader has worked for the company since he was an apprentice on the factory floor in his youth. He knows everything there is to know about the machinery, the widgets and the products his company has and makes. He is far more interested in how machine number 35 will get back up and running again, or how long it might take a helicopter to get from its base to the scene of an incident, than he is in how the crisis is playing externally. This sort of leadership encourages the crisis team to get involved in the detail, rather than to think about the big picture strategy and the future.

The consensus-builder This leader cannot bear to make decisions until everyone is on board. He needs to feel that none of his colleagues oppose the course of action that is to be taken. This, however, is not leadership at all. Leadership involves making decisions, even when there is no consensus.

The bank manager This leader is always conscious of money, but only in the short term. Rather than thinking about the long-term financial damage if reputation is lost (loss of customers, expensive new regulation, share price collapse), he is worried about the short-term cost of withdrawing products, overriding insurance policies, bringing in the best advisers and so on. You might even hear this leader ask his finance director: 'What will this spend mean for bonuses at the end of the financial year?' The answer to that question should be: 'If you carry on with that mindset, you won't have a job at the end of the financial year.'

The recluse Scared of the media, this leader finds excuse after excuse for not communicating during the crisis. His favourite phrase is 'let's just wait until... ', followed by, for example, 'the results come through/we take a view from the local team/we start to get media calls' and so on. The result is an inwardly focused crisis response, which leads to a reactive and defensive standpoint when the media start to take an interest. This leader thinks his anti-communications strategy will ensure the organization retains control, but, in fact, it risks the crisis being owned by others.

It would be easy to list the characteristics required for good leadership – controlled, empowering, listening, perceptive, decisive, inspirational, brave, strategic and so on – but very few people possess all these traits. What is important is for those senior executives who may be put in a crisis leadership position to have the opportunity to understand their own style and to work on any aspects of their style that they – and their peers – believe can be improved.

Personification of crises

The question of leadership is becoming more and more important in the changing external context in which crises are managed. All of us, encouraged by the media and their emphasis on human interest and celebrity, increasingly personalize corporate crises, looking for a face to fit the situation. We may be looking for heroes, but more often we are looking for villains.

An interesting example of the 'personification of crises' was the Shell reserves scandal that hit the oil giant in early 2004. When Shell was forced to announce that it was significantly downgrading its own estimates of its oil reserves, the reaction of the business media and Shell shareholders was one of fury. For various reasons, the company crisis soon became inextricably linked with Chairman Sir

Philip Watts. Within a one-week period, dozens of articles delivered a negative assessment of his performance. To take a snapshot of the media coverage, UK newspaper articles on 27 January 2004 led with opening words such as 'Sir Philip Watts, Chairman of Shell, was again under fire today… ' (*Financial Times*); 'The position of Sir Philip Watts as Chairman of Shell has been further weakened… ' (*The Guardian*); 'The Chairman of Shell, Sir Philip Watts, suffered a fresh setback yesterday… ' (*The Independent*).

Coverage became extremely personalized, with the press mounting what has since been referred to as the 'Where's Watty?' campaign to find the absent Chairman. The main reason for this personalization was his decision not to make the important reserves downgrade announcement himself. This was then exacerbated by a perception that Sir Philip was the personification of Shell's allegedly uncommunicative and bureaucratic management style. A *Sunday Times* article stated that Sir Philip 'reeks of all the worst elements of the company – patronizing, bureaucratic, secretive, lumbering and under-performing'.[9]

This personalization of the issue by the media may have been grossly unfair, but fairness in a case such as this is, unfortunately, irrelevant. As Chapter 2 explained, the media thrive on conflict, especially if it involves 'victims' and 'villains'. The media successfully characterized the story as a battle between the Chairman (the villain) and angry Shell shareholders (victims). The media were clearly not going to give up until they got their man, and Sir Philip Watts eventually (and perhaps belatedly) resigned. The negative press coverage for Shell almost immediately started to wane.

There are other examples of business leaders who have stepped down as a public sign of penance and change. The media tend to report this as a positive sign that they, and other stakeholders, have managed to make a difference, and it often results in a 'bounce-back' for shares. For example, Steve Case resigned as Chairman of AOL Time Warner in January 2003, saying that the company needed to focus on the challenges it faced, rather than a debate about its leader: 'I would love to serve as Chairman for many years to come, but I believe stepping down is in the best interests of the company', he said.[10] The share price started to recover after he resigned.

Phil Condit, CEO and Chairman of Boeing, resigned in December 2003 'to put the distractions and controversies of the past behind us'. Although he was not implicated in the corporate scandals that had rocked the company, analysts were reported by the media as saying that this would help the company clean up its image. *The Guardian* described this as 'an honourable exit'.[11] And in the political arena, the scandal that engulfed the UK Transport Secretary Stephen Byers after his adviser had said that 9/11 was 'a good day to bury bad news' did not abate until he reluctantly resigned in May 2002. In his resignation letter, he wrote: 'What is clear to me is that I have become a distraction from what the government is achieving.'[12]

Senior executives sometimes have to fall on their sword in order to protect the company from perceived underperformance or poor management. If senior executives see themselves as defenders of the company's reputation, they must be prepared to take whatever actions are necessary to fulfil this role, including resignation. This does not have to be admission of failure and it should not be done until all other avenues have been explored and the case for continuity fully communicated. Put simply, if the leader's resignation will kill a reputation-damaging story that will otherwise not go away, the leader should resign.

The leader as hero

But leaders do not have to be villains. Leaders can be heroes too. Former New York City Mayor Rudolph Giuliani is, at the time of writing, running for president in the United States, in large part thanks to his perceived hero status after his leadership role in the immediate aftermath of the terror attacks on New York and Washington in September 2001. In fact, the terror attacks that have happened in major cities around the world in recent years provide interesting comparisons in crisis leadership.

If you examine the attacks on New York, Madrid and London, you will see that the very similar terrorist incidents produced very different outcomes for political leaders. In the United States, whilst Giuliani emerged as a hero, President Bush did not come out of the 9/11 attacks as a good crisis leader (and also failed to display leadership qualities after the hurricanes of 2005). It was expected that a forthright and bullish leader such as President Bush would immediately take the lead in this situation. To a certain extent, he did. With the President declaring his 'war on terror' on the evening of the attacks, his approval ratings soared and were recorded at 90 per cent shortly after the attacks.[13] And yet the President's absence in the crucial early hours of the crisis (understandably, he had been whisked away to a safe location) meant that the media hero was created elsewhere. It was Giuliani, whose understated but solid leadership fitted the mood of the moment, who took the role of hero. Giuliani was, until the attacks of 11 September, a fairly controversial figure with a colourful private life – not what you might consider presidential material. He was also a fairly powerless 'lame duck', coming to the end of his term of office. And yet, following the events of 11 September 2001, he was hailed not just as the Mayor of New York but as 'America's Mayor'.[14]

Nobody emerged as a hero or trusted leader after the attacks in Madrid. The attacks at Atocha station in March 2004 led to the sitting government's defeat at the polls a few days later, thanks to a bungled response, which involved a crisis management cardinal sin: speculating on the cause. The Spanish government said too much too soon and, when it was shown to have been wrong, its credibility was shattered.

Soon after the attacks, police officials informed the government that explosives often used by Basque separatist group ETA were found at the blast sites, which, along with other suspicious circumstances, led them to suspect ETA involvement almost immediately. Although there was no direct evidence pointing to ETA involvement, the group had been caught with a large amount of explosives some months previously, which looked like preparation for a big strike. But, according to a report issued by The European Strategic Intelligence and Security Center (ESISC), the Spanish Intelligence Service had concluded that the attack was instigated by an Islamist terrorist group on the morning of the bombings. They had, however, been ordered by the government to deny the Islamist lead and insist that ETA was the only suspect.[15] The government went so far as to send messages to all Spanish embassies abroad ordering that they upheld the ETA version. President José María Aznar allegedly called a number of newspaper directors personally to ask for their support of this version.[16] This did not prevent some of the smaller Spanish outlets running with the news that Al-Qaeda was behind the attacks, a theory that was given almost immediate credibility when a van used and abandoned by the bombers was recovered containing not only detonators but also Islamic audio tapes.[17]

It is completely understandable why a government such as Aznar's would feel pressured into finding the culprits behind such an act of evil immediately. After the Oklahoma City bomb, President Clinton was under huge pressure to lay the blame on Islamic terrorists. But his caution was justified, as it emerged that the bomber was a solitary white American. It is politically understandable for a party that takes a hard line on ETA to want to lay the blame with this terror group. But the results spoke for themselves. Public opinion turned against the ruling Popular Party and the socialist opposition won a surprise victory at the following weekend's elections.

British Prime Minister Tony Blair emerged from the July 2005 attacks on London's transport infrastructure not as a hero, but as a statesman. At the time of the attacks, he was in Scotland for a G8 summit. On learning of the atrocities, he flew down to London to chair a meeting of the cabinet office crisis committee, COBRA, and then flew back to Scotland to carry on with the summit. The message was that he cared and was in control, but was not going to be distracted by terrorists. His actions and words matched the mood of the country, and helped prevent what many commentators thought might be a backlash against the Iraq war.

Three cities, three crises and three very different outcomes. The lesson for crisis management is that leadership matters. One further case study below shows good leadership in action.

Branson does a Bishop

Another example of good crisis leadership came in February 2007, when Virgin boss Richard Branson turned a potentially reputation-damaging incident – a crash involving a Virgin Trains service – into an example of best practice crisis communications.

Branson's leadership echoed that shown by Sir Michael Bishop in 1989, when the airline he ran faced a major crisis. British Midland, a UK-based airline that at the time was not a well-known brand, was perceived to have managed a plane crash in the East Midlands very well, in large part thanks to the leadership shown at the beginning of the crisis by Bishop. On 8 January 1989, a British Midland Boeing 737 flying from Heathrow to Belfast crashed near the M1 motorway, killing 47 people and seriously injuring 10. The aircraft crash-landed short of East Midlands airport after engine malfunction. Unlike previous aviation disasters, when media comment was left to anonymous company spokespeople, British Midland Chairperson Sir

Michael Bishop offered himself openly for media enquiries. On his way to the scene of the accident, Bishop gave live radio and television interviews from his car phone. He gave these interviews when he had no knowledge about the cause of the accident or whether there had been casualties. He told of his concern and sympathy for the victims' families and kept the media constantly updated about the inquiry. British Midland suffered no subsequent loss of traffic on the Heathrow–Belfast route and maintained its prior level of growth.

Bishop said of his handling of the crash: 'I suppose it was a bit of a gamble, but I had given the matter of what to do if we had a crash a lot of thought over the years and it seemed to me the best way to tackle the crisis when it actually happened.' He added that he had 'probably set a new style for dealing with such crises'.[18] *The Daily Telegraph* described Bishop's handling as 'a classic lesson in how to handle a catastrophe', adding that 'a weaker man might have hidden behind the need for an official inquiry. Instead, Bishop displayed a masterful understanding of adversity leadership: sympathetic, transparent and helpful.'[19]

Eighteen years later, on the evening of Friday 23 February 2007, a Virgin train travelling from London to Glasgow derailed and crashed at Grayrigg, near Kendal, Cumbria, killing one person and injuring five. The train was travelling at approximately 95 mph and was carrying about 120 people. Eight out of the nine carriages derailed and slid down an embankment.

Analyzing from the outside the crisis management overseen by Sir Richard Branson, there is little to criticize. At a press conference at the scene of the crash, he was visibly emotional and every comment he made seemed positive, complimentary and dignified. Sir Richard Branson even said that he 'took his hat off' to Network Rail (the company created by the government to manage the railway infrastructure) for being 'dignified' in accepting responsibility for the accident. Branson had cut short a family holiday to attend the scene of the accident and visit the hospitals treating the injured. He hailed the train driver as a hero: 'He's carried on sitting in his carriage for nearly half a mile, running the train on the stone – he could have tried to get back and protect himself but he didn't, and he's ended up quite badly injured. He is definitely a hero. In the sober light of day we will have to see if he can be recognized as such.' Branson also praised the design and robustness of the train, saying that an older train would have resulted in 'horrendous' injuries and mortalities.

On Monday 26 February, Network Rail announced that the suspected set of points were in fact the cause of the accident. One of the stretcher bars was not in position, two others were fractured and bolts were missing. It also confirmed that there was no evidence that the train was a contributing factor. Branson's words had been backed up by the facts.

A closer analysis shows that Branson's intervention was a high-risk strategy. First, he speculated about the cause of the crash, blaming the points before the official investigation was anywhere near being so concrete. Second, he broke ranks with other stakeholders by stepping over the media lines that Network Rail, the British Transport Police, the Rail Accident Investigation Board and others had agreed and upheld. Third, he made a hero out of one of his own people when others, such as the emergency services and a local farmer who pulled people out of the wreck, perhaps had a better claim to being the media hero (just how much control can a driver have over a train that has left the rails anyway?).

But Branson's gamble (whether it was a conscious gamble or not) paid off. The media were kind to Virgin and its leader. *The Independent* newspaper questioned whether the rail industry was learning from its past mistakes, but praised Branson: 'Sir Richard Branson still deserves credit for returning from his holiday early and visiting the scene of the accident, something that chief executives still too rarely do in such circumstances.'[20] During a PR conference, *The Independent* editor-in-chief Simon Kellner described Branson's handling of the crisis as 'genius PR'. He added that 'Branson took the story away from being an institutional and public disaster and made it one about the heroism of the train driver.'[21] Branson's response is likely to be remembered in crisis management best practice for as long as Bishop's.

In crisis management, there is more focus than ever before on leadership. There is consequently more pressure than ever before on leaders. Branson, Giuliani and Bishop all demonstrated that leaders can emerge from crises with their reputations enhanced. But not all organizations will be so lucky as to have a natural crisis leader. For any organization that is taking its reputation seriously, investment in understanding and improving crisis leadership is time well spent.

Crisis management – an action plan for change

This book is about how reputation management in the new world order is about much, much more than crisis preparedness. PR commentator Paul Holmes hits the nail on the head in his regular newsletter when he argues that:

> Many companies are preparing for the wrong kind of crisis. Too many executives still think of crises as catastrophic events – airplane crashes, explosions at plants, product tamperings. But corporate reputations are unlikely to be damaged by such crises, unless the company is shown to have been negligent or its response was somehow inadequate. Far more damaging are the kind of chronic crises that arise over time, often a direct result of a company's culture or management.[22]

These chronic risks to reputation (which I will call issues, but that is just another matter of terminology) are dealt with in the next chapter.

If I was to take issue with Paul Holmes, I would say that an 'inadequate response' to a crisis is a pretty big 'unless'. True, corporate reputations can be saved, but a sudden event or development in which the consequences are great and the scrutiny high is still one of the biggest reputation risks an organization will ever face. And, it is one of the most stressful and memorable times of any corporate executive's career.

Poorly managed crises hit the bottom line hard (the *Valdez* oil spill cost Exxon more than US$15 billion) and can ultimately kill a company (the Lockerbie disaster and its reputational consequences proved to be the final straw for Pan Am). Getting it right, on the other hand, can have its positive effects. Crises can also be seen as opportunities. They may not feel like it at the time, but the long-term goodwill generated amongst stakeholders by a well-managed crisis can be significant.

To conclude, my top 10 recommendations for developing corporate best practice in crisis management are listed in the following box.

Top 10 recommendations for best practice in crisis management

1. *Prepare your leaders* It is their moment to shine or fail. They won't succeed just because they are senior. Help them get it right through good training and self-awareness of leadership strengths and weaknesses.

2. *Simplify the crisis manual* Make it as user-friendly and accessible as possible, and be creative with ideas for ensuring key crisis personnel have the core elements of the process and structure with them at all times.

3. *Understand powers and limitations* Crisis management can fall down if people either don't feel they are empowered to take the right decisions, or they overstep the mark. Ensuring that teams and individuals understand their powers and limitations is fundamental to a good crisis response.

4. *Focus on competence* People are crying out for training and development in areas where they feel inadequate or uncomfortable. Crisis management requires boldness and confidence, and competence equals confidence.

5. *Watch the team dynamic* This is the other part of behavioural crisis management. Teams that know each other, and have rehearsed together, perform better when the occasion demands.

6. *Communicate early and often* Crisis team members need to understand how the crisis will be seen and reported by the media. It may seem 'unsavoury', but crises are played out in the public theatre, and the company must play its role to the best of its abilities.

7. *Don't forget your own people* Remember the stakeholder priority list? Your employees come very high on it, so don't assume that they know what is going on or are not emotionally affected. They may need counselling; they certainly need communication and leadership. And they are potentially powerful advocates.

8. *Own the crisis* All crises have stakeholders, some of whom think they have an important role to play in the management of the crisis. Focus on the stakeholders that

matter, and build constructive relationships with the other players.

9. *Practise, practise, practise* There is simply no substitute in crisis preparedness for having been put through your paces on a regular basis.

10. *Show, don't tell* Don't just tell the media and stakeholders that you care, show them. Don't just tell them that you are doing everything you can, show them. Emotion and visuals are far more effective than empty commitments and platitudes.

Notes

1. See Regester, M and Larkin, J (2005) *Risk Issues and Crisis Management,* Kogan Page, London.
2. *Wall Street Journal* (25 March 2005) 'BP's Safety Procedures Draw Scrutiny'.
3. *Financial Times* (25 March 2005) 'BP Must Repair Its Tarnished Reputation'.
4. At the time of writing, the bad headlines continue for BP. A headline in the *Financial Times* on 20 March 2007 read: 'BP Safety Culture Under Attack', reporting comments from the head of the US Chemical Safety and Hazard Investigation Board and reminding readers of the conclusions of the Baker Panel report.
5. *The Independent* (17 January 2007) 'Spillages and Scandals: An Annus Horribilis BP Would Like To Forget'.
6. Mitroff, I (2005) *Why Some Companies Emerge Stronger and Better from a Crisis,* Amacom, New York.
7. Report of the 7 July Review Committee, paragraphs 1.15 to 1.17.
8. Kotter, JP (1996) *Leading Change,* Harvard Business School Press, Boston, MA.
9. *Sunday Times* (11 January 2004) 'Shareholders Can No Longer Be Sure of Shell'.
10. *The Guardian* (14 January 2003) 'Case Admits Defeat at AOL Time Warner – Merger Maker Bows to Investors and Quits'.
11. *The Guardian* (2 December 2003) 'An Honourable Exit'.
12. BBC Online (28 May 2002) 'Stephen Byers Quits Government'.
13. US News.com (2002) 'One Year'. Available at: http://www.usnews.com/usnews/9_11/articles/911opener.htm. Accessed on: 13 June 2007.

14. Attributed to Oprah Winfrey (23 September 2001) *Newsday* newspaper.
15. European Strategic Intelligence and Security Center (17 March 2004) *Briefing Note, Post Incident Report: Attacks on Madrid.*
16. *Democracy Now* TV programme (23 November 2004) 'Remembering March 11: The Madrid Bombings and Their Effect on Spanish Government, Society and the Antiwar Movement'.
17. *BBC News* (11 March 2004) 'Spain's PM Vows to Catch Killers'.
18. *PRWeek* (4 March 1993) 'PR Helps Bishop Fly – British Midland'.
19. *The Daily Telegraph* (14 February 2007) 'Why it is Better to Lose Money Than Your Reputation'.
20. *The Independent* (26 February 2007) 'A Safety-First Approach'.
21. *PRWeek* (2 March 2007) 'Independent's Kellner Lauds Branson for Response'.
22. Holmes Group (January 2006) *The Holmes Report*, London. Holmes Report newsletters are published online at: http://holmesreport. com.

5 Issues management – shaping the agenda

Issues management has been the little brother of crisis management for too long. I would challenge any organization to examine all the present and future risks to their reputation and come to any conclusion other than that it is under constant threat from a wide range of issues. Organizations of all shapes and sizes are struggling with actual and potential issues from global warming to local restructuring, from ethical supply chains to product quality.

However, it would be wrong for me to present this as some sort of competition between issues management and crisis management, as if the two were mutually incompatible. That's not the case at all. The two disciplines have the same ultimate end: to protect, and enhance, reputation through the potentially bad times. They should therefore go hand in hand as part of reputation risk management: one looks at the acute risks, the other deals with the chronic risks. But, for whatever reason, this joined-up reputation risk management rarely happens.

As the audit results showed in Chapter 1, issues management is seen by some communication departments as: 'It's just what we have to deal with every day. Things crop up; it would be better if they hadn't cropped up; they're not crises; but they need managing.' In my view, managing these blips is not issues management. That's just life in any normal organization. An issue is something different. It is something that is identified as a genuine actual or potential risk to reputation; something that, if not properly managed, might drag on or escalate to be something that is as damaging to reputation as a badly managed crisis. The main difference is that, with issues management, you have more space and time. It is, perhaps, the space and time that give comfort. There is more urgency about a burning building than a building that is possibly contaminated with asbestos. With the former, scrutiny and pressure are high and (unless you manage it very badly) short-lived; with the latter, there may be no external interest at all. You can be in the middle of a difficult issue and still head home on time every night.

But the comfort that this space and time provide is false comfort, because the consequences are potentially worse in the case of asbestos contamination than a fire. Many of the most famous case studies in reputation management are issues. The McLibel case was an issue – it dragged on, day after day, for years, with occasional peaks of external interest. The Brent Spar case was an issue. The Nestlé baby milk controversy was an issue (more on that below). Monsanto's debacle when introducing genetically modified crops to Europe was an issue. The 'AIDS drugs in Africa' case study was an issue for pharmaceutical companies. The health scares about mobile phone handsets and masts were/are an issue.

Some might argue that the case studies above are crisis case studies, that they may have started off as issues but they became crises after a certain level of interest and reputation damage had been reached. This could be true of some of them, but not all of them. To the best of my knowledge, Nestlé never convened a crisis management team on the baby milk issue.

Some issues do become crises. Or rather, in the terminology I think is more helpful, some chronic risks can become acute risks. The Shell reserves issue as described in the previous chapter was a chronic risk for some time: the e-mails that became public showed that it had been identified as a concern internally for some 18 months or so before the announcement that elevated it immediately to an acute risk. At that point, I imagine crisis committees were convened and the risk was managed in a very different way so, yes, it had become a crisis.

I won't labour this particular point, as it boils down once again to terminology. The point is that an issue does not have to somehow morph into a crisis for it to become damaging to reputation. If you wait until a crisis is declared before taking a stronger interest, you may have waited too long to save your reputation.

Issues management – difficult in theory

Issues management is 'difficult in theory' for the same reasons laid out in the previous chapter explaining why crisis management is 'easy in theory'. Or, rather, for the opposite reasons. First, whereas crisis management is about trained and competent people implementing a plan that has been prepared and rehearsed in advance, issues management is harder to systemize. No company that I know runs 'issues management exercises' to practise and hone their issues management skills. One transport company did run what they called an 'issues-based crisis', which was an honourable attempt at running an exercise for senior management using an elevated chronic risk as the scenario rather than an acute risk. It apparently worked well in that it showed senior management what can happen when issues escalate, but the urgency and professionalism of the participants' response only really kicked in when the facilitators introduced elements more familiar to crisis management (ie, when people started getting hurt).

Second, there is no 'window of goodwill' in issues management as there is in crisis management (or certainly in the management of big physical crises). If you watch the television news tonight and you are confronted with corporate issues such as redundancies, land contamination, working practices in developing countries and sugar/fat/salt content in popular foods, you would not be in a state of shock. There would be no sense of sympathy for everyone involved or a spirit of 'we're all in this together'. Your first reaction, if you believed what you saw and heard, would more likely be outrage. This is why organizations need to get issues management right from the very beginning.

There is a second emotional dimension to this. One of the most common definitions of an issue is 'the gap between expectations and performance'. This is nearly right, but not quite right. In the hostile external climate in which companies are operating today, many people actually *expect* companies to get things *wrong*. The change in attitudes in the developed world since the advent of the anti-globalization movement means that many people now expect the worst of companies. Indeed, they are almost looking out for companies to get it wrong. Some even want companies to get it wrong, so they can rejoice in the incompetence of companies and use it to reinforce the world view to which they have subscribed. This, in part, is a consequence of the failure of companies in recent years to stand up for themselves and take on their opponents.

Expectations are therefore low. Demands, on the other hand, are extraordinarily high. There is no tolerance at all of corporate failure. Companies now need to be like politicians: devoid of human failings. So the public is not saying to companies: 'We look up to you and expect a lot of you, and if you don't meet those expectations you will have an issue to manage.' People are increasingly saying: 'We look down on you and expect you to make a mess of things, and we are scrutinizing your every move to see if you do, but we will not tolerate failure.'

In the developing world, the attitude tends to be very different. An example would be a pharmaceutical company that wants to recall a product from the market because of a small misprint on the label. Assuming the misprint does not put patients at risk, the recall is likely to be perceived in a developing world country as an example of a company going above and beyond its obligations. The company will have exceeded expectations. In many developed countries, the same recall is more likely to be seen as 'another corporate mistake' and an example of how companies fail to meet demands.

The dynamic of issues management today is far more complex than 'the gap between expectations and performance'.

Categorizing and prioritizing issues

With the modern corporate collision course so fraught with issues, some sort of assessment and prioritization system is needed. As with the earlier example of the financial service company's preparation for an AGM, many big companies now have folders of issue management material containing dozens if not hundreds of issues. They can't all be as risky as each other, can they?

First, there is a difference between categorization and prioritization. To avoid having dozens of completely different issues in one prioritization model, I would urge organizations to categorize before they prioritize. The categories I use are:

1. *Corporate issues*   These are the issues arising from the running of the company and its products and services and would include corporate governance issues, product quality concerns, values, performance and so on (the Nestlé baby milk issue and the Shell reserves issue both fit here).
2. *Global issues*   These are the big issues of the day, which are not just about an individual company and would include, for example, ethical sourcing, environmental issues and obesity.
3. *Local issues*   These are the issues with a defined affected group, such as local redundancies, contamination at one site, a planning application for new premises (the siting of mobile phone masts and the Waitrose case from Chapter 3, for example).

There is obviously some overlap, as there is with any categorization system, but most issues fit fairly obviously into one category rather than another. There is overlap here too with the social responsibility agenda, which is dealt with in the next chapter. A company's environmental impact is now firmly considered to be part of the 'social responsibility' area, although clearly it is an issue too. The acid test for whether something straddles the issues/CSR divide is whether it is likely to feature in the ever-lengthening corporate responsibility report.

Which of the three issue categories above causes the greatest reputation risk? Logically, the order should be the sequence in which they appear above. Corporate issues should come first because they call into question the very purpose of an organization's enterprise, the integrity of its people and the quality of its products/ services. Global issues should come second because they attract the most publicity in the most markets, even though they affect many companies rather than just one. Local issues should come third because they only affect a small (and therefore more manageable) constituency. But one of the consequences of the changing and hostile external world is that local issues can very easily become national issues or even international issues.

And then from categorization to prioritization. There are many different ways in which companies categorize issues, but they are all broadly similar. Many are risk matrix systems that map the severity of consequence (impact) against the likelihood of it happening. So, if something has high consequences and stands a good chance of occurring, it appears in the top right-hand corner of the matrix and is given more resources than an issue that is fairly low impact and has only a slim chance of materializing into something significant. That seems simple enough.

Another favourite is the 'bull's-eye' model: a series of colourful concentric circles within which identified issues are pushed further and further towards the centre depending on various criteria. The positioning is often based on scores, but sometimes just based on the intuition of those charged with updating it on a regular basis.

How do you prioritize something that is based so often on perceptions and emotions rather than facts? Take, for example, an international site reassignment programme (turning industrial land into residential land for sale). Say there are 100 sites that are to be reassigned and there is an expectation that the programme could cause controversy. How do you prioritize the work? By size of site? By the amount of work needed to be done to the site? By the perceived attitude of the local community? By the stance of the local media? By the presence of organized residents' committees? By the size of your business in the country? By the proximity of local elections? By all of the above, in a scoring and ranking system? The latter is probably the answer but, with so many unpredictable potential trigger points, it is almost impossible to allocate issues management resources in a meaningful way. But prioritization has to happen somehow, because no business can allocate the same resources at the same time to 100 sites around the world.

Categorization and prioritization have to be done. Models and tables help stimulate and clarify thinking, and provide logic to otherwise instinctive decisions. But, as this is a very inexact science, do not lose sight of those potential issues that you have put in the bottom left-hand box of the matrix or the outer ring of the bull's-eye model. It does not take much in the new world order for these issues to jump suddenly from nowhere to being significant reputation risks.

Beyond this, the four key points I want to highlight in this issues management chapter are:

- issues management is as important as crisis management, but requires different skills and tools;
- local issues can now have global consequences;
- issues management is about agenda control;
- global issues need (uncharacteristic) long-term thinking.

Issues management is as important as crisis management, but requires different skills and tools

Walk into a crisis room and you will see that most people know where to start. They might not be as competent as they could be, they might be lacking in confidence, they might be relying too heavily on the dusty manual in front of them, but there is at least some measure of organization. Walk into the first meeting of a group brought together to manage an issue, and the same sense of organization is rarely there. This is a problem, but it is also an opportunity. It is a problem because senior management in any organization should want to feel assured that issues are as well-handled as crises. After all, issues are as potentially damaging to reputation as crises. It is an opportunity because any organization that wants to manage its issues better has a blank page on which to create an excellent fit-for-purpose system.

Many companies will claim to have an issues management system, but even some of the more mature issues management systems are little more than systems that help identify, categorize, prioritize (see above), escalate and monitor issues. Very few of them provide meaningful guidance on actually how to manage the issues. Managing an issues management system is not the same as managing an issue.

In this short section, I focus primarily on systems management, as this is where the biggest gap lies. However, as many organizations are currently struggling with issues identification, this too needs to be addressed.

In brief, identification should be seen as a cultural matter rather than one of process. This comes back to the advice in Chapter 3 about ensuring that reputation is genuinely at the heart of the organization. This is a matter for education (explaining to people across the organization how unmanaged issues develop into threats to reputation), people management (explaining to employees that spotting and escalating an issue will not increase scrutiny or workload for them) and loyalty/reward ('far from putting you in the spotlight for identifying an issue, we want to show you our gratitude for thinking about the reputation of the entire organization'). It is vital to foster a corporate culture in which people at all levels can feel confident to raise issues, escalate them and know that their vigilance is appreciated. Any system for identifying issues is entirely dependent on creating this culture. It is the next step – managing the issue – that is the one requiring more systemic thought. It is easier to spot an issue than to do something about it.

The first trap to be avoided is creating issues management procedures that mirror crisis management procedures. As we have already seen, the two disciplines require very different approaches. The last thing you want to do when confronted by an issue is to turn it into a crisis yourself, by taking the organization's most senior people away from their day jobs and getting them to focus on something that should be handled at another level. By virtue of their involvement, the issue is already on a path of escalation, from which it may be difficult to pull back.

Furthermore, issues management can and should be systemized in order for it to be taken seriously, but it must not be strangled by process. It would be a disaster if an over-engineered issues management system was introduced into an organization just as the management of crises was moving away from complex process towards behavioural and emotional preparation. This would be like using yesterday's tools for one discipline to address today's needs in another.

So how do you find the right balance? The best systems encourage the user to make the right decisions. Often, however, users see the system as either a security blanket or a straitjacket. If they do not have the confidence and competence, they look at the system for comfort in the hope that the system itself will manage the issue. If they do feel that they have the confidence and ability to manage the issue, they can see the system as an obstacle to achieving what they think they can achieve.

The analogy I use for a good system is a golf caddy. A golf caddy points you in the right direction, helps you choose the right tools (clubs), helps you manage outside influences (weather), advises you on how to manage the situation ahead of you (the course) and gives you the confidence-boosting pep talk. But he or she does not take the shot. You do. Ultimately, the best clubs, balls and guidance are useless if the person taking the shot is a hopeless hacker.

The same goes for an issues management system (or any system). It must be there to assist, not to instruct; to make things easier, not more complex; to encourage excellence, not stifle initiative. Many issues management systems, to continue the golfing analogy, just get you to the course, give you a set of clubs and leave you to it: they tell you that the course needs playing and that you must spend your time doing it, but then they leave you to your own devices. Some then put so many obstacles in the way, including about 20 other players who think that it is their job to take the shot, that you risk failing to get off the first tee.

There is a tendency in issues management to bring more and more people into the team. This tendency is much greater than in crisis management, where it is usually recognized that decision-making needs to be done by a small body. This is helped by the fact that the decision-makers are usually physically in a crisis room, and any more than 12 people round the table will feel unmanageable. In an issue, the teams are often virtual and can become huge. I was involved in an issue in 2006 that started off with about eight people in the loop but, within three weeks, I counted 37 people on the e-mail distribution list and 24 people dialling in to one conference call. Extending the team is not a sign of 'involving the best and the brightest to solve a problem'; it is a sign of insecurity.

A good issues management system must encourage ownership, empower decision making and provide helpful guidance and tools. In that order. To that end, organizations should focus on ensuring the lines of responsibility are clear and fair, that individuals who are tasked with managing a particular issue are trained and confident, that they know their powers, limitations and reporting requirements, and that they have access to a toolkit if they need it. If they then make mistakes, 'the system' cannot be blamed.

Obviously, it is far more complicated than that, and it is for organizations to work out the logistics depending on their individual profile, issues, people, structure and culture. But if they tackle issues management with 'ownership, empowerment and guidance' top of mind, they will be off to a good start.

Local issues can now have global consequences

A colleague was recently doing some work for a quasi-public-sector organization that was seeking advice on communicating a controversial decision about land redevelopment. There was clearly going to be a large 'aggrieved community' that was unlikely to take kindly to our client's plans. The client asked the question: 'Could this go national?' My colleague replied: 'National? For all I know it could go international!'

There was, in fact, very little chance of the story getting much interest outside of the local town or region, but the point my colleague was making is that the boundaries in issues management are now extremely porous. There is now always a small chance that a local group – or even an individual – using new technologies, employing the right tactics and targeting the right audiences can get attention almost anytime and anywhere. The power of the individual, the power of campaign groups and the power of the media in today's world can all come together to turn seemingly the most benign of issues into an international cause.

Companies need to be aware of this, and indeed most global organizations are painfully aware of it. Any multinational that has had its AGM interrupted by individuals or groups purporting to represent a distant local community, unsatisfied product users or exploited workers will know that these challenges need extremely sensitive handling. It is the David versus Goliath stories such as these that can overshadow the larger issues or that provide human interest context to the larger issues.

The challenge that this brings to companies is in spotting and managing issues in territories that used to be considered 'outposts' but that are now as important to the corporate whole as any other. Furthermore, this challenge extends beyond the corporate borders into the wider supply chain. This is not easy, as it requires a certain amount of standardization of action and communication across an organization that will comprise many different cultures and styles. The problem is: how can you answer all questions about all issues across the whole global company without taking central control of issues management? And, if you do think that issues need central command, how do you impose a global way of managing them to protect your brand without introducing an overcomplicated process that might stifle rather than encourage action?

There are many different answers to these questions, but there is no one solution. The most honest answer is that there is no infallible global issues management system that will reliably spot and manage issues at the right level of the organization and with absolute consistency across the world. But this does not satisfy the modern demands on companies.

And, to make matters worse, these demands are conflicting. On the one hand, there is criticism of companies that try to standardize everything and turn the diverse world into a world of bland corporate conformity. On the other, there is criticism of companies for having 'double standards', that is, doing something in one way in one country, and in another way in another country. And, as with the Waitrose example in Chapter 3: yes, they can have it both ways.

So, the answer to the question about managing local issues in a global organization is that it can never be answered, as it is asked in so many different, and sometimes conflicting, ways. It is the premise of the questions that companies need to address before they can hope to answer them through policy or process.

Issues management is about agenda control

A consequence of managing issues by complex process or by replicating crisis management procedures is that the response can become defensive. There is a temptation to spot problems with everything and to react accordingly. In a way, this is not a bad thing in that it encourages people to be alert to problems and to think 'from the outside in'. But, on the other hand, it can sometimes result in a siege mentality or a negative mindset about matters that should generally be a matter for positive internal and external communication.

The terms of debate on issues are too often dictated by others. We live in times when, in much of Western society, the announcement of excellent profits is a risk to reputation. In the communications battle about whether successful and profitable businesses are a good thing or a bad thing, businesses have not only failed to win the argument, they have in the most part failed to join in. This is because companies have taught themselves to be cautious in the new external climate. The overall corporate mentality is that 'no news is good news'. So much so, that you get the following examples.

Imagine an airline that is changing its route timetabling. The change is in response to passenger demand and reflects the statistics for where and when customers are using the airline. The airline has calculated that 96 per cent of passengers will benefit from the amended timetable and wants to ensure that this good news is communicated. But instead of going to a consumer PR company and/or advertising agency to publicize the change, it comes to a reputation risk management consultancy. 'We'd like you to help us manage the issue', it says. What issue? This is a good news story for passengers. Yes, it has a downside in that 4 per cent of passengers will be inconvenienced because the half-empty flights that it uses are making way for routes to other destinations. But it is still good news. Concentrate on the downside, and your reputation is controlled by the 4 per cent, the good news for the 96 per cent will be lost and the media will have their 'victims and villains' story. Concentrate on the good news and your reputation is potentially enhanced.

Imagine a global mining company that is planning to develop a new mine in a small community in Australia. The company's first planning application is met with a small local campaign by a group of 12 community members who are against the development. Taking fright at the local sensitivity, the mining company withdraws its application. The majority of the community then petitions the company to return and to bring with it much-needed jobs, wealth and opportunity. Over 500 people turn up at a town meeting to show their support. Emboldened, the company reintroduces its planning application. Eighteen months later, the group of 12 has grown to a group of 20 and is running a decent campaign amongst local politicians and the media. The company is spending a huge amount of management time dealing with the issue, and the development of the mine has consequently stalled. The company feels its reputation is once again on the line and is considering withdrawing. What happened to the 500 people who made a proactive statement of support two years ago? Why are they and their needs being ignored because a small minority are more organized and more vociferous?

The above examples are fictional but based on truth, and there are plenty more examples out there of companies that have allowed issues to be managed on the terms of others. One well-known example of an issue that rumbled for years (and is still rumbling) on an agenda set by a tiny group of activists is the Nestlé infant formula issue. This is one of the most famous issues management case studies of all time, but few authors have really got to the bottom of it. The usual case studies accuse Nestlé of ignoring the issue for too long and hoping it would go away, of sticking by a product that had serious ethical issues attached to it or of failing to understand the strength of feeling about such an emotive subject. There may be some validity to all of these criticisms, but the bigger problem was that Nestlé managed the issue for too long in the territory of its opponents. A small network of campaign groups set the agenda for this debate, and Nestlé danced to their tune, as the case study below shows.

Nestlé – baby killers or life savers?

The issue of child nutrition is an emotive one. Few people would argue with the fact that breastfeeding is the best, cheapest (it's free, after all) and safest way for mothers to feed their babies. But since the dawn of the human race, not all mothers have been able to breastfeed their babies. Whether from a medical condition, poor education or necessity to work, some mothers have either chosen to or had no other option but to seek alternatives to breastfeeding, even for very young babies. Unfortunately, the foods that mothers have substituted for breast milk (unpasteurized cow's milk, rice water, fruit juices and so on) have been prone to contamination and have led to infant death.

Henri Nestlé developed infant formula products in the 19th century. Even then, the inventor recognized that breastfeeding is best for babies, and that his product was only suitable for mothers who had to find a substitute. About 100 years later, Henri Nestlé's products started to become controversial.

The issue started in the mid-1960s, when a child nutritionist, Dr Derrick B Jelliffe, developed the idea that the infant formula industry was responsible for infant mortality in the developing world. This provoked little reaction, with most serious bodies (including the UN Protein Advisory Group) promoting the use of infant formulae amongst vulnerable groups. However, the issue did not completely disappear and, in the early 1970s, some other child nutritionists started to support the condemnation of infant formula companies. Nestlé invited people to come to their headquarters in Switzerland to learn more about infant formula. A representative of campaign group War on Want visited and subsequently wrote a publication called *The Baby Killer*. This then was picked up by another organization that wrote a campaigning pamphlet called *Nestlé Kills Babies*. Not long thereafter, boycotts started in various markets and the issue took hold.[1]

The basic argument of the anti-Nestlé campaigners seems to be as follows. Nestlé is a huge multinational that makes money from infant formula. Nestlé (and some other infant formula manufacturers) aggressively market these breast milk substitutes in the developing world. Mothers who would otherwise be breastfeeding start to use infant formula. They mix the powder with contaminated water, which puts the baby at risk. Furthermore, the babies get 'hooked' on formula and, as the mother's milk dries up, mothers have no choice but to pay for more formula, dilute it to save money and put their baby's life at greater risk. Approximately 1.5 million babies die every year from unsafe bottle-feeding.

This argument is flawed on so many different levels. Most mothers in the developing world who do use breast milk substitutes do it out of necessity. If they have a job and support a family, they are highly unlikely to get good maternity leave like mothers in the developed world, so they need to return to work quickly. Infant formula gives them an option to do that. Those mothers who do use formula are usually urban mothers who can afford the product and who have access to clean water (or know how to make water safe). The only product recognized by the World Health Organization as a suitable alternative to breast milk is infant formula. The vast majority of the 1.5 million babies that die from 'unsafe bottle-feeding' are the unfortunate ones who do not have infant formula or another nutritional alternative to breast milk in the bottle.

Infant formula is a life saver, not a baby killer. But this message never came in a clear and confident way from Nestlé in the early days of the issue. Instead, Nestlé engaged with the concerns raised by the activists and developed internal guidelines limiting advertising and promotions or anything that could be deemed to be encouraging mothers to stop breastfeeding in favour of using its products. Shortly thereafter, infant formula manufacturers participated in the creation of the WHO Code of Marketing of Breast Milk Substitutes. Whilst this Code ended some of the boycotts, it did not stop the issue completely.

There is nothing wrong with the Code and its intentions. The fact remains, however, that the Code is a symbol of all the possible problems associated with infant formula. It is based on an assumed negative: that, without the Code, Nestlé and other infant formula manufacturers would be harming babies. It establishes a set of stringent standards that no global company can ever guarantee it can meet 100 per cent of the time. For example, the Code bans incentives such as product promotions on infant formula, but how can a company like Nestlé ever totally eliminate the possibility that an independent shop owner in India will do a two-for-one offer on its infant formula? The Code therefore invites people to police it, and the anti-Nestlé campaigners happily do this because it keeps the issue firmly on their territory.

In the late 1990s, Nestlé started to communicate better with its stakeholders. It is here that I should declare an interest, as I worked as a consultant to Nestlé for a short period at this time. The focus of the communication was the company's compliance with the Code. For example, on some occasions when allegations were levelled by campaigners that a Nestlé product or employee was breaking the Code, it was investigated and the results communicated to various supposedly interested parties. Literature was developed that set out the allegations made against the company, and the truth as the company saw it. Again, these were well-intentioned initiatives showing compliance with an international set of standards, but part of a reactive and defensive strategy that ensured the issue remained on the territory of the anti-Nestlé groups.

It was only from 1999, when Nestlé started to address student union meetings in the United Kingdom (some student unions had long boycotted Nestlé products), that the company started to regain the initiative and take control of its reputation. These meetings, although sometimes heated and fraught, were a success. In fact, it was a real turning point as it allowed Nestlé to start communicating more on its own territory. For the first time, some students and campaigners were hearing the real history and importance of infant formula products. And they were hearing it from Nestlé employees from the developing world, some of whom were themselves working mothers.

The Nestlé infant formula issue has not completely gone away. It is too institutionalized in some NGOs for it to vanish any time soon.

There are still some charities that refuse to meet with Nestlé, and at least one charity has turned down a huge cause-related marketing deal from the company.[2] There is still a hardcore group of activists who have a political interest in – and indeed whose jobs depend on – hating Nestlé. But the issue is now far less troublesome for the company than it was even 10 years ago. The main reason for this is that the company started to show its commitment to the product, articulate its belief in the product and communicate on its territory. Nestlé replaced, at least partially, an attitude of 'We can prove that we are not as evil as you think we are' with one of 'We have an important, potentially life-saving product here that we are proud of.'

The Nestlé experience throws up some interesting points about the creation of internal standards and policies. Many companies, when faced with issues that arrive from allegations or incidents, go down the route of adopting internal standards or signing up to external standards or, as in Nestlé's case, codes of practice. This is fine, as it goes: it is admirable to set targets and to commit to sticking by them. But, again, so many of these standards – even those, such as the OECD guidelines on how multinationals should operate in the developing world, based on initiatives by well-meaning organizations – are premised on a negative: 'We do not take bribes' is an invitation to discuss bribery and corruption.

Give me a commitment from a multinational company such as 'We do not take bribes' and give me a month and the resources, and I'll give you a well-argued document explaining where and how it does take bribes. Companies know that, so they water down the commitments to platitudes such as 'it is our policy never to take bribes. Where bribery is proved, we will take action.' This is less convincing, as it opens the door to the possibility of bribes and ties the company to sacking people who do. Incidentally, who does the proving?

If you are a global company with tens of thousands of employees and significant operations in various developing world countries, I would wager a fair sum that someone in your company has given or taken a bribe in the last 12 months. Does that make you a bad company? Of course not. Should you do something about it? Yes. Will it ever be fail-safe? No.

This is not to say that living by these codes is a bad idea (and, of course, the Sarbanes–Oxley Act of 2002[3] turns much of this into requirements anyway); it is merely to say that if you sign up to something that says 'we will not use suppliers who pay their staff less than US$10 per day' or 'we will not tolerate bribery', you invite people to find faults and accuse you of hypocrisy or mismanagement. And, you are protecting your reputation on tricky terrain.

Issues management is not just about managing the issues that come your way. It is about controlling the issue and controlling the agenda. If you have an issue, own it. Challenge the premise if you need to, and don't blindly accept the territory on which the issue is managed. It's your reputation, so grab issues positively and take the upper hand in the battle to shape it.

Global issues need (uncharacteristic) long-term thinking

Companies, like governments, think short term. Money, unfortunately, is at the root of this particular problem. Governments find it difficult to assign funds to long-term problems when it could be spent on short-term wins. Companies need to satisfy short-term financial demands before thinking about the longer term. The average CEO and the average government minister probably have about the same expectations for job longevity, which drives them to think in chunks of two to four years rather than two to four decades.

Climate change is the obvious example of an issue that needs long-term thinking. Governments seem to find it easy to impose taxes to deal with the perceived future threat of climate change, but find it more difficult to spend the money raised on environmental initiatives. And, companies find that the markets like them to talk the language of environmental concern, but still demand short-term profit generation above all else. With the possible exception of NGOs, the other players also think and act in the short term.

Individuals may also feel concerned about the possibility of climate change affecting their future prosperity and lifestyle, but are not entirely happy about being penalized through the tax system for their own contribution to carbon emissions. NGOs do perhaps have the freedom to think long term, but their short-term and long-term interests collide: they need to talk about the long-term issues in order to secure short-term membership and funding.

Whether you believe the science that tells us that the climate is changing and humankind is to blame or you believe the science that tells us that the climate is changing only marginally and humankind is a negligible factor, the whole issue has undoubtedly become one that all large organizations need to address with long-term strategy. The case study at the end of this chapter looks at how three companies – Exxon, Wal-Mart and Virgin – have changed their positions on climate change.

But this is not the only long-term issue that governments and companies are collectively failing to address. The case study below is on energy security. It is an issue that has a cycle of short-term thinking, which one of the two main players – government and the oil industry – needs to break.

Energy security: long-term issue, short-term agendas

With oil reserves steadily depleting, more investment needs to be made in new energy sources to ensure security of supply in the future. Energy security is an issue that all energy companies are grappling with, but the levels of investment are as yet unimpressive. Why? This is a classic long-term issue that has been characterized by short-term thinking by both governments and companies. Both are acting rationally, but neither is willing to break the cycle of short-termism.

The massive investment required by industry will not be generated unless private companies can expect an acceptable return given the risk. But, with the level of political risk high, the investment climate is anything but stable. So, companies choose not to invest at the sort of levels they need to. Why is the investment climate unstable?

Governments in both the developed and the developing world have, in the last few years, either threatened action or taken action against the wealth of energy companies. In the United States, the CEOs of the oil majors were called before the Senate in 2005 to explain record industry profits. This built on a climate of distrust of the oil companies, which were perceived to have benefited from global risks such as terrorism and natural disasters. Put simply, if terror attacks and hurricanes push the price of oil up, the oil majors benefit. In the United Kingdom, the Chancellor imposed a tax on oil companies in late 2005, which was widely seen as a 'raid on profits'. The profitability of TOTAL became an issue in the French presidential elections of 2007. And we have seen how the political tide has turned against oil companies in Latin America.

The vicious circle of short-term issues management therefore looks something like this:

- The energy industry feels that global risks and the uncertain climate created by governments mean that long-term investment is high risk.

- The global risks and events cause the price of oil to rise, boosting energy profits.

- In the climate of high risk, companies protect their 'winnings' and shareholders get good returns – this pleases the markets.

- Governments, acting on a sense of unfairness that oil companies have derived wealth from risks or crises, highlight the 'evils' or 'grotesque wealth' of the energy sector and introduce new or higher taxes on industry.

- Companies feel vindicated in their belief that the investment climate is risky, and further batten down the hatches.

This may seem like rational self-interest on the part both of governments and industry, but it is hardly enlightened self-interest and it is not long-term issues management. It is also risking the long-term wrath of people, who are both energy consumers and voters.

Who can break this cycle of short-termism? Industry is best placed to do this, as in this scenario it is the 'villain', whilst governments can more easily play the role of 'hero'. If a crisis or prevailing sense of risk (resulting from natural disasters and tension in the Middle East, for example) creates 'winners' when there are so many social and economic 'losers' from the crises themselves and the resultant high oil prices, this breeds suspicion, resentment and conflict. The public does not need further encouragement to mistrust or resent the energy industry, and governments do not need further encouragement to impose new taxes in an effort at realignment.

So, if the battle of reputations is being won by governments, it is for the energy companies to make the first move. To do so, they will need to do what does not come naturally to companies: play the long game. It will be a brave CEO who risks the wrath of the markets and ups the ante on this issue with massive investments in new energy. But when the long-term consequences of short-term thinking are as high as they are in this instance, bravery is needed.

Companies are reluctant to take the lead on long-term issues, for many very good reasons. To take the lead is often a financial and reputation risk. On the other hand, as we have seen, companies are permanently under the microscope and increasingly made the whipping boys for some of the big ticket issues of the day. Companies, when they feel the pressures of scrutiny and blame, are too quick to lie low and allow the mud to stick. Attack might sometimes be the best form of defence. Exposing the hypocrisy and inaction of others, whilst showing that you are able and willing to make the first overtures towards a long-term solution, can be a better strategy both reputationally and financially.

Long-term thinking may be uncharacteristic now, but it is vital if companies are to protect themselves and their stakeholders in key debates. This, once again, is about regaining the reputation initiative.

To conclude this chapter on issues management, my top 10 recommendations for developing corporate best practice in this discipline are listed in the box below.

Top 10 recommendations for best practice in issues management

1. *Don't treat issues management as secondary to crisis management* The language of issues may be less emotive than that of crises, but the outcome of a badly managed issue can be as bad as – or worse than – a badly managed crisis.
2. *Get the categorization system right* A list of 100 issues will just confuse people. Break them down into categories that make sense for your organization.

3. *Prioritize resources, but don't forget the rest* Any issue, given the right combination of external triggers, can be catapulted quickly from bottom of the list to top.

4. *Don't kill issues management with convoluted systems* The more time people spend managing the system, the less time they spend managing the issues.

5. *Focus on competence* As with crisis management, competence is the key. If staff are skilled, confident and empowered, the systems are far more likely to operate well.

6. *Beware the institutionalized issue* Are there issues in your organization that have drained resources for years and on which people's jobs depend? There shouldn't be. Good issues management should lead to resolution, not stagnation.

7. *Keep issues management teams tight and empowered* Yes, get the right people, representing the right functions, round the table, but 30-strong issues management teams will barely manage themselves, let alone the issue.

8. *Control the agenda* Don't allow others to set the terms of the debate. Always manage issues from the front.

9. *Beware of promises you can't keep* The moment you make a corporate commitment, you will have people monitoring its implementation. This can add fuel to the fire.

10. *Think long term.* Encourage your organization to take a stand on long-term issues and prove that it can make a difference. Courageous companies and leaders can shape the future.

Business responds to climate change: Wal-Mart, Exxon and Virgin

How do you solve an issue like climate change? Especially when, according to one respected international newspaper, 'Climate change could be the next legal battlefield: compensation claims for man-made environmental damages would make the tobacco sector payouts look small.'[4] This case study looks at how three of the world's biggest and most successful companies – Wal-Mart, Exxon and Virgin – have changed their stance on climate change in the last few years.

Climate data shows that the earth is experiencing a warming period. There is no conclusive single theory for why the climate is changing, but the scientific debate on the matter could not exactly be described as 'healthy'. Indeed, so powerful is the growing perception that humans have caused climate change through CO_2 emissions, that the matter is 'closed' in many people's minds. Two key developments reinforced this 'closure' – the release of the Al Gore film *An Inconvenient Truth* and the publication of the Stern Review.[5]

So, if the perception has firmly taken hold that people are to blame for the problem, who needs to provide the solution? The spotlight for change is on everyone, but perhaps there is special expectation from industry. Because of this, some companies have stopped questioning the science and/or making only token efforts to 'do their bit', and have instead joined the mainstream.

Wal-Mart

Wal-Mart is the largest retailer in the world. It is the largest grocery seller and toy retailer in the United States. It is also the largest private employer in the United States and Mexico. Wal-Mart has more than 1.8 million employees worldwide, 7,000 stores and wholesale clubs across 14 countries, and has a net income standing at US$12.178 billion.

The 'Beast of Bentonville' has never been known for its environmental credentials but, at the end of 2005, CEO Lee Scott announced a series of startling plans for the business to become more sustainable and environmentally friendly. It is currently embarking on these initiatives:

1. Investing approximately US$500 million annually in technologies and innovation to reduce greenhouse gases at its stores worldwide by 20 per cent over seven years.

2. Designing and opening a retail outlet that is 30 per cent more efficient and will produce 30 per cent fewer greenhouse gas emissions within four years. Wal-Mart says it will favour suppliers who do the same.

3. Reducing solid waste from US stores by 25 per cent within three years.

4. Increasing truck fleet efficiency by 25 per cent over three years, doubling to 50 per cent within three years.

Lee Scott also has aims to turn the company into one that runs on 100 per cent renewable energy and produces zero waste, and estimates that the above initiatives will lead to savings of US$310 million per year. Scott said the company's new stance was due to a combination of personal and business motives: 'It just became obvious that sustainability was an issue that was going to be more important than it was last year and the years before... We recognized that Wal-Mart had such a footprint in this world, and that we had a corresponding part to play in sustainability.'

Wal-Mart has received wide recognition for its new stance, but it inevitably still draws criticism. Wake-Up Wal-Mart, a group backed by the United Food and Commercial Workers union called it 'a publicity stunt meant to repair a faltering public image'. In a comment piece about the sustainability of capitalism, UK newspaper *The Guardian* said rather sarcastically: 'All hail Wal-Mart for imposing a 20 per cent reduction in its own carbon emissions.'[6]

But critics of Wal-Mart should consider the influence that the organization could have with its millions of employees and customers. Climate change is still primarily a debate in the middle classes. As Scott says: 'The shift toward sustainable lifestyles has thus far been stratified based on income or education.' Wal-Mart could play a huge role in democratizing sustainability.

ExxonMobil

According to *Fortune Magazine*'s 'Global 500', ExxonMobil is the largest corporation in the world. Much like Wal-Mart, ExxonMobil is considered by many as a juggernaut of capitalism, aggressively consuming resources and getting rich in the process. The company has traditionally been seen as a foe to the environment, an image that stems in large part from the 1989 *Exxon Valdez* tanker disaster, which resulted in 10.8 million gallons of oil being spilled in Prince William Sound, Alaska.

Within the hydrocarbon industry, ExxonMobil has perhaps been the least receptive to climate change. Former Chairperson, Lee Raymond, said as recently as 2005 that Europe needed a 'reality check' over its commitment to the Kyoto Protocol.[7] The company courted controversy by funding organizations that cast doubt on the mainstream science of climate change. The company has been targeted relentlessly by environmental and anti-corporate activists. Several monitoring groups have been set up, including Expose Exxon, Campaign ExxonMobil and Exxon Secrets. The latter was set up by Greenpeace and lists well over 100 organizations that it claims have been given money by the oil company.[8]

While the industry has been addressing the issue of climate change, led by BP's 'Beyond Petroleum' rebranding, ExxonMobil has therefore been positioned by its opponents as a climate change denier. In an era where questioning the role of human-made greenhouse gases in climate change is politically and socially unacceptable, ExxonMobil felt increasingly isolated and exposed.

The company has recently discreetly indicated a softening of its views. Whereas Wal-Mart's entrance to the climate change debate was accompanied by fireworks and astonishment, ExxonMobil nipped in the back door, hoping not to be noticed. The announcement didn't come from Chairperson and CEO, Rex Tillerson, but from the Vice President of Public Affairs, Kenneth Cohen. In January 2007 he was widely reported as saying: 'We know enough now – or, society knows now – that the risk is serious and action should be taken.' He confirmed that ExxonMobil had 'quietly' started meeting with leaders of various environmental groups. Regarding the company's position on climate change, Cohen told *Fortune Magazine*: 'We should be putting ourselves on a path, as a society, to reduce emissions in ways that are cost-effective and sustainable.'[9]

In February 2007, Rex Tillerson confirmed ExxonMobil's shift by saying that: 'It is prudent to develop and implement sensible strategies that address these risks while not reducing our ability to progress other global priorities, such as economic development, poverty eradication and public health.' In the same speech he offered a robust defence of the oil industry, saying that there is no clear alternative to oil and gas in the near future: 'I'm no expert on biofuels. I don't know much about farming and I don't know much about moonshine. There is really nothing (Exxon) can bring to that whole (biofuels) issue. We don't see a direct role for ourselves with today's technology.'

Virgin

With trains and planes part of his business empire, Sir Richard Branson was never a vociferous advocate of the 'global warming is caused by humankind' theory, but never one to do things by halves, Branson has been courting publicity since late 2006 for his new environmental agenda. At the Clinton Global Initiative (an annual conference hosted by Bill Clinton) in September 2006, Branson said that Virgin would be investing US$3 billion (£1.6 billion) to fight global warming over the next 10 years. The money used to fund this will come from the profits of his travel companies, Virgin Atlantic and Virgin Trains. It will be invested in renewable energy technologies via his investment unit Virgin Fuels. Branson said that we must 'rapidly wean ourselves off our dependence on coal and fossil fuels'. In February 2007, Branson appeared with Al Gore to announce a US$25 million (£12.8 million) prize for the scientists who could invent a way of extracting greenhouse gases from the atmosphere. He claimed it to be the largest such prize ever offered.

Has Branson's change of tack made a difference? Yes it has. A survey in *The Times* has shown that, although airlines are generally criticized by the public for failing to do enough on climate change, the airline identified as having made the biggest contribution to minimizing the environmental impact of flying is... Virgin Atlantic.[10]

Notes

1. Potted history from Green, S, Jones, S and Sidgwick, C (July 2006) The Nestlé issue from an evidence-based midwifery perspective, *British Journal of Midwifery*, **14** (7).
2. Breakthrough Breast Cancer declared it had rejected a £1 million deal on ethical grounds. See *Ethical Performance* magazine, July 2004.
3. A US federal law passed after a number of major corporate and accounting scandals, such as Enron and WorldCom, which imposes strict reporting standards on all US public limited companies.
4. *Financial Times* (14 July 2003) 'Climate Change Could Be Next Legal Battlefield'.
5. Stern, N (2007) *The Economics of Climate Change*, Cambridge University Press, Cambridge, UK.
6. *The Guardian* (2 February 2006) 'It's Capitalism or a Habitable Planet – You Can't Have Both: Our Economic System is Unsustainable by its Very Nature. The Only Response to Climate Chaos and Peak Oil is Major Social Change'.
7. Commondreams.org (18 February 2005) 'Exxon Chief Calls for Kyoto Reality Check'.

8. See http://www.exxonsecrets.org/. Accessed on: 13 June 2007.
9. *Fortune Magazine* (26 January 2007) 'ExxonMobil Greens Up Its Act'.
10. *The Times* (April 25 2007) 'Most Britons Believe that Airlines are Failing to Clear the Air'. When asked which airline is doing the most to minimize the environmental cost of flying, 62 per cent of respondents said Virgin, with BA on 20 per cent and other airlines far behind.

6 Social responsibility – your initiatives on your initiative

There are, I suspect, very few things about which anti-business campaign group Corporate Watch and I agree, but the first sentence of its report on corporate social responsibility (CSR) in 2006 is one of them: 'CSR evolved as a response to the threat anti-corporate campaigns pose to companies' licence to operate.'[1]

Some may disagree with this sentence, preferring to think that companies embarked on the CSR journey out of some sort of Damascene conversion to social justice or sudden realization that it was the right thing to do. But, for me, CSR is very much part of reputation risk management. It is another manifestation of the corporation under fire. It was and is a defence mechanism against the collision course of the hostile external world. And you can tell, because CSR is, on the whole, managed reactively, defensively and entirely on the territory of others.

If corporate social responsibility as it is understood and managed today was about enhancing reputation, companies would have stopped doing it by now, because it doesn't work. The biggest spenders on CSR are the biggest and most successful global companies, and they are still under fire all the time. CSR seems to make little, if any, difference. So why do they do it? There are two main reasons.

First, companies are afraid that today's social responsibility issues will turn into tomorrow's lawsuits, and think that by engaging with the CSR agenda they are limiting future liabilities. This is particularly true of food companies (obesity claims) and companies with high carbon emissions (climate change claims) and/or operations in the developing world (human rights claims).

Second, they have always done it. CSR is not a new concept. Companies have been doing it since well before the term was invented. Since the early days of corporate philanthropy in the 19th century, companies have historically 'given something back'. Whether this was done through a financial donation (as has always been particularly popular in the United States) or creating whole towns for workers (Lever Brothers with Port Sunlight and Cadbury's with Bournville in the United Kingdom), good companies have always been keen to be good corporate citizens. Being a good corporate citizen is good for business because it builds respect amongst employees and others.

If the preceding paragraphs seem inconsistent, let me explain. Being a good company is not a new concept and is a 'no-brainer' in that good companies are more likely to be popular and popular companies are more likely to be successful; the term CSR is a new(ish) concept that describes a set of initiatives, standards and expectations that reflect a prevailing external agenda that is sceptical of business.

The difference between being a good company and engaging in the CSR agenda of today is an important one, because this chapter strongly criticizes the CSR agenda and the way in which companies have engaged with it, but at the same time encourages companies to be good businesses and good corporate citizens. I therefore do not agree with the hard-line fans of Milton Friedman[2] who think that all corporate spend on 'unnecessary' activities such as community investment or charitable giving is money stolen from shareholders. Good companies are good neighbours in the communities in which they operate, and are good citizens of their host societies and of the world at large. This helps them increase revenues and profitability, returning money to shareholders. So, it is surely in the long-term self-interest of shareholders for companies to invest in being seen as 'good companies'. But the fundamental message of this chapter is that CSR, as currently understood and implemented, is not the vehicle for companies to prove that they are good.

What is CSR?

For a concept that is understood in so many different ways by companies and other organizations, CSR is actually defined fairly consistently. The European Commission's definition is as good as any: 'CSR is a concept whereby companies integrate social and environmental concerns in their business operations and in their interaction with their stakeholders on a voluntary basis.'[3] Like most definitions, this one stresses the voluntary nature of CSR and the fact that it is about integrating social and environmental matters with normal business operations. Some like to capture neatly the integration of financial performance, environmental performance and social performance into the phrase 'triple bottom line' reporting. Others merge the concept of sustainability into CSR, stressing that sustainable businesses are those that take account of environmental and social needs as well as financial ones.

Companies have embraced CSR wholeheartedly. No global company based in the developed world would dare have a corporate website that has no mention of social responsibility. The vast majority of global companies produce a hard-copy CSR report too. And 900 companies have signed up to the UN Global Compact, which has promoted 10 universal principles on responsible corporate citizenship since it was founded in 2000. The concept of CSR, like the whole concept of reputation, is everywhere.

But what about CSR in practice? What does it actually look like? To repeat what was found in the audit mentioned in Chapter 2, it seems that CSR in practice involves a mix of the following:

- brand-led cause-related marketing initiatives, which openly position a brand alongside a good cause or charity (Tesco's 'Computers for Schools' initiative in the United Kingdom, for example);[4]
- independent corporate social investment, not linked to a particular brand and often involving the giving of time and expertise as well as money (for example, Standard Chartered Bank's 'Seeing is Believing' campaign);[5]
- reporting on compliance, whether to external or internal standards of business (eg, emissions, bribery and so on);[6]

- reporting on issues, such as how the organization is responding to concerns it has received or major issues of the day (eg, human rights, local environmental concerns and so on);
- donations.

All of the above are admirable, and are legitimate ways in which businesses can be – and be seen to be – good businesses. To lump them all together under the umbrella of CSR, however, is extremely unhelpful.

As with previous chapters, this chapter on CSR cannot hope to cover more than a few aspects of this huge and fascinating area of corporate reputation risk management. It will therefore cover the following five main points:

- CSR is about business, but not controlled by business.
- CSR does not shield companies from reputation risk.
- CSR reports are a waste of time and trees.
- The concept of corporate citizenship is more helpful than that of CSR.
- Performance matters more.

CSR is about business, but not controlled by business

Perhaps the most important point to make about corporate social responsibility is that, although it has 'corporate' in the title, it is a concept that has been shaped by and controlled by governments and NGOs. It is a term that is now synonymous with 'ethics' and is used in such a way as to suggest that, without it, businesses would be unethical and irresponsible. To me, well-worn statements such as 'we are committed to corporate social responsibility' have a negative undertone to them. They make being a good business sound like a chore, or something that a company has reluctantly signed up to. They are based on a negative perception that businesses have allowed to take hold: that companies are not a force for good in the world unless they somehow change their ways using the banner of CSR.

Were you to have a discussion about terms commonly associated with CSR, which words and phrases might crop up? 'Investment' and 'community support'? Perhaps. 'Standards' and 'commitments'? Certainly. 'Sweatshops', 'environmental damage', 'bribery', 'corruption'? Probably. Of course, CSR is about *preventing* all of those bad things, but the point is, that it is defined with these very negative concepts in mind.

How has this happened? Most of Chapter 2 is about how companies have ended up on the back foot in terms of their reputations, so this chapter will not go over that ground again. Specifically, with the term CSR, anti-corporate campaigners have successfully turned it into a stick with which to beat companies. As Bryan Cress, senior adviser on CSR and globalization at the CBI, told *The Guardian* in 2003: 'CSR has been hijacked by NGOs, so that businesses are expected to do things they just can't do. The starting point seems to be that businesses are guilty, therefore they ought to solve the problems of the world and deliver all kinds of social goods. But there is no sense of the roles and responsibilities of other players.'[7] And NGOs have hijacked the premise of CSR to such an extent that the term is now also used against companies. For example, having persuaded businesses to buy into their version of CSR, some campaigners are now saying that CSR is a sham. A Corporate Watch report states that 'CSR enables business to propose ineffective, voluntary, market-based solutions to social and environmental crises under the guise of being responsible.'[8] Corporate Watch is not a 'mainstream' NGO, but this quote reflects the view of many anti-corporate activists. In a similar vein, a spokesperson from Friends of the Earth has been quoted as saying: 'You will see a lot of advertising from these companies highlighting their green credentials but this is all about trying to boost the morale of their staff and ultimately it's superficial.'[9]

Organizations such as Corporate Watch and Friends of the Earth believe that if companies are not socially responsible, they are bad, but if they do CSR, they are covering up their badness. Either way, they use the language of corporate social responsibility to attack companies and everything that they stand for. In addition, companies, rather than turning their various initiatives into positive reputation enhancement, have generally allowed this negative connotation of the term to take hold. Companies have, in the words often used by PR agencies, 'engaged with the agenda' of CSR as it is seen and promoted by others. One of the risks of taking this submissive approach is that one of the most crucial parts of the definition of CSR – that it is voluntary action by companies – will be eroded. Indeed, it is already under increasing threat from governments.

Summarizing the responses it received to a consultation paper on CSR, the European Commission reports:

> Trade unions and civil society organizations emphasized that voluntary initiatives are not sufficient to protect workers' and citizens' rights. They advocated for a regulatory framework establishing minimum standards and ensuring a level playing field. They also insisted that in order to be credible, CSR practices could not be developed, implemented and evaluated unilaterally by businesses, but rather with the involvement of relevant stakeholders.[10]

Of course they did. They are not really interested in corporate voluntary initiatives or companies being 'good businesses' at all; they are interested in changing the way the corporate world works altogether.

The Commission went on to report what other stakeholders had contributed to the consultation exercise, before drawing its own conclusion:

> Adopting CSR is clearly a matter for enterprises themselves, which is dynamically shaped in interaction between them and their stakeholders. Nevertheless, as there is evidence suggesting that CSR creates value for society by contributing to a more sustainable development, there is a role for public authorities in promoting socially and environmentally responsible practices by enterprises... CSR practices and instruments will be more effective if they are part of a concerted effort by all those concerned towards shared objectives. They should be transparent and based on clear and verifiable criteria or benchmarks.[11]

In other words, CSR should be a matter for corporate voluntary action... but we want to standardize it. European companies have reached their leadership position on social responsibility and sustainability issues without this sort of intervention from the EU. For the EU to involve itself in this arena would be supremely unhelpful and ironic. As Steve Hilton and Giles Gibbons write, the EU 'has done as much as any other institution on earth to keep developing countries in poverty by refusing to dismantle its trade barriers... It is just laughable that this of all organizations has the nerve to lecture anyone on social responsibility.'[12]

The EU's equivocal stance is a reflection of a trend that is seeing corporate responsibility gradually shifting from the realm of voluntary action to the realm of standards and harmonization.[13] Many nation states are also implementing, or considering, laws that will effectively turn aspects of CSR into requirements. Forms of mandatory disclosure have been implemented in France, Denmark and the Netherlands. In the United States, a Corporate Code of Conduct Act was considered, which would have required US-based multinationals to disclose on various issues.[14]

In the United Kingdom, turning voluntary social responsibility initiatives into mandatory reporting sparked a fierce debate. The Chancellor of the Exchequer announced in November 2005 that he was scrapping plans to introduce a requirement for all listed companies to produce an operating and financial review (OFR) – an annual narrative statement on future risks and opportunities, including environmental issues. Friends of the Earth took the Treasury to the High Court in January 2006, arguing that the Chancellor had failed to consult before making the U-turn. The Treasury, fearing the publicity of a court case, introduced a replacement known as the Business Review. This 'compromise' also requires companies to provide a narrative of their performance against a range of financial and non-financial key performance indicators, but it waters down the OFR's need for verification of environmental performance, for reporting on social issues and for statements about future plans on environmental issues.

Interestingly, some businesses are so firmly on the CSR bandwagon that they opposed the scrapping of the OFR, even though it had been positioned by the Treasury as a pro-business, anti-red-tape decision. This was not, in my view, an example of turkeys voting for Christmas, but rather a reflection of the fact that CSR has become so entrenched that some think it might as well be made a legal level playing field. 'At least we'll know where we stand', one rather haunted-looking company 'CSR officer' said to me.

Turning CSR into regulation would be a disaster. It would be hugely counterproductive, as it would turn the concept of doing 'good business' into little more than a dull box-ticking exercise. However, calls for this are only going to grow louder unless companies change the debate on CSR. Corporate acceptance of the terminology of CSR as presented by others is a mistake. To sit back and allow it to be turned into regulation or legislation would be an even bigger mistake.

CSR does not shield companies from reputation risk

As a reputation risk management strategy, CSR has a marginal effect. Certainly in comparison with the value of management time that is spent on CSR, the return on the investment in terms of reputation is minimal. Examine the website or the CSR report of practically any global company and you will find laudable initiatives paid for by the private sector. Coca-Cola, for example, has created the 'Global Water Challenge' with Procter & Gamble, CARE, UNICEF and others. The project is aimed at improving sanitation, hygiene education and access to clean water in developing countries. But Coca-Cola still gets activists outside its AGM waving banners about how the company 'destroys farmers' lives', and the media are still happy to join in the chorus of criticism. A little bad news about Coca-Cola will always get more column inches than a lot of good news.

In Africa, Asia and other tropical regions, new cases of lymphatic filariasis (also known as elephantitis) – an incurable disease that puts a billion people at risk of disabling deformities – may be eliminated by 2020 in large part because of a billion-dollar donation by GlaxoSmithKline. However, this does not stop campaigners opposing the company on many other grounds.

There is a paradox here. The more successful your company, the more likely you are to be in a financial position to invest in meaningful CSR. However, the more successful your company, the less likely your CSR programmes are to be appreciated by the NGOs and governments that dominate the agenda. Of course, no company should be immune from criticism just because it has spent some of its profits on a social initiative, but a company might at least hope that the initiatives it implements under the banner of CSR will build a sense of trust and confidence, which will in turn be of benefit to the company when a reputation risk arises.

Unfortunately, companies hoping to build credit in the reputation bank through CSR will be disappointed. With its 'Computers for Schools' initiative, Tesco has had one of the United Kingdom's most famous and respected CSR programmes of the past decade, but the company is still routinely criticized for its success and profitability. And the case study below shows how Starbucks was still on the receiving end of (unfair) criticism for its coffee purchasing policies despite the many related CSR schemes it has in place.

Starbucks and the Ethiopian beans

Starbucks has built a reputation for being a socially responsible company that pays higher prices for its coffee to ensure fair trade with developing world producers. It is also widely acknowledged that the company has created trickle-down benefits for other businesses. As *The Economist* points out, the likes of Starbucks have cultivated a taste for good coffee, a trend that has seen small independent coffee shops prosper too.[15]

Starbucks has engaged wholeheartedly with the CSR agenda. Here are just a few of the many 'CSR initiatives' that Starbucks has undertaken:

- In 2001, Starbucks introduced a set of coffee sourcing guidelines with the support of Conservation International (CI). The guidelines reward farmers and suppliers that meet quality, environmental, social and economic criteria with financial incentives and preferred supplier status. Suppliers must submit an application to the programme, which is required to be verified by an independent third party. Starbucks has received over 90 applications for the programme.

- Starbucks runs initiatives to provide farmers with access to affordable credit, which helps them keep financially stable without resorting to selling at low prices.

- Fairtrade and other 'Commitment to Origins' whole bean coffees are available to buy in Starbucks stores. Since forming an alliance with TransFair USA in April 2000, Starbucks has purchased nearly 900,000 kilos of Fairtrade-certified coffee.

- Since 1998, Starbucks has worked with Conservation International to promote sustainability in coffee-growing countries. Through CI's Conservation Coffee programme, Starbucks encourages the production of coffee using traditional cultivation methods that protect biodiversity and provide improved economic opportunities for coffee farmers.

- The Starbucks Foundation has a mission to 'create hope, discovery and opportunity in communities where Starbucks partners (employees) live and work'. To date, the Foundation has given US$12 million to more than 700 youth-focused organizations in the United States and Canada.

Perhaps most importantly, Starbucks pays its growers an average of 23 per cent above coffee market price for their beans.

None of the above CSR initiatives seem to help Starbucks with certain audiences. A website called ihatestarbucks.com is still devoted to opposing the coffee company's plans and existence. It seems that every time Starbucks tries to open a new store in affluent neighbourhoods, it faces opposition; it has even had coffee shops trashed by anti-capitalist campaigners. When issues arise, the company's CSR programmes rarely feature in NGO opinion and media reporting.

In October 2006, Oxfam UK accused Starbucks of attempting to block a move by the Ethiopian government to trademark the names of three of its most famous coffee beans in the United States. The NGO said that Starbucks asked the National Coffee Association (NCA), the trade association of US coffee companies, to block the country's bid. Oxfam claimed that, by blocking the trademarks, Starbucks was denying Ethiopia earnings of £47 million per year. Starbucks denied this and claimed that the trade body contacted Starbucks over the issue, not the other way round. Robert Nelson, head of the NCA, confirmed this, saying that the trade association was against the move because it would damage Ethiopian farmers economically. He said that the Ethiopian government had been badly advised and the move could result in the government setting coffee bean prices unreasonably high, resulting in fewer exports.

In December 2006, Oxfam posted a clip on the video-sharing website YouTube that criticized the company's policies in Ethiopia. The video has received almost 50,000 hits. On 16 December, Oxfam organized the 'Starbucks Day of Action', which encouraged people to protest at branches of Starbucks around the world.

Starbucks did not manage the issue particularly well, and there was a public admission of misjudgement from Alain Poncelet, Vice President of and Managing Director of Starbucks Coffee Trading Company. He said it was 'very clear to us that we have not engaged as much as we should have in East Africa. We all agree that we are looking for the same results and that the farmer should be the one benefiting. We are not in a position to tell the Ethiopian government what to do. We are a coffee company; we do not set the rules.'[16]

Who do people believe in this debate? Who is more likely to have the interests of coffee farmers at heart? Starbucks, a company that seems transparent and committed to CSR and that pays over the odds for coffee beans from its suppliers, or the government of Ethiopia, which ranks 130th in Transparency International's Corruption Perceptions Index? Let's look at the evidence.

One of Starbucks' hometown newspapers, the *Seattle Post-Intelligencer*, said that the Starbucks CEO was playing 'Russian roulette' with the brand: 'It's ironic that Starbucks' anti-development stance will likely lead to a greater impact on profits than any increase in commodity prices the company might encounter was it to support Ethiopia. Ethiopians cannot dig themselves out of poverty unless they are allowed to participate meaningfully in the value chain. Let's hope Starbucks allows them to do so.'[17] Seattle's other daily newspaper, *The Seattle Times*, said the dispute had 'rattled' Starbucks' image.[18] The *Houston Chronicle* condemned the company: 'Shame on Starbucks, whose revenues in 2005 were $6.4 billion, for trying to strong-arm a country whose entire gross domestic product is $6 billion.'[19] The company also received over 70,000 customer letters about the matter.

If, as seems to have been the case, most people instinctively believe that Starbucks was in the wrong, this says something about how successful anti-corporate campaigners have been in denouncing global businesses and how unsuccessful companies like Starbucks have been in defending their reputations through CSR programmes.

The most extraordinary example in recent times of an entire industry engaging with social responsibility initiatives and responding to social concerns only to find themselves rewarded with more regulation is the food industry and the obesity debate.

Obesity – CSR unrewarded

Obesity, if we are to believe the hype, is a major threat to the health of the developed world's people and economies and many countries are feeling the need to 'do something' about it. In the United Kingdom, the debate about obesity has been steadily growing for some years, and it reached fever pitch in 2006. In August 2006, the UK Department of Health said that if no action was taken, 13 million people in the United Kingdom would be obese by 2010.

Health Secretary Patricia Hewitt used the figures to highlight that obesity was an individual rather than a collective burden: 'The government's got a responsibility to make it easier for people to make healthy choices for themselves. But at the end of the day, it's up to each of us to decide what we eat, what we drink, how much exercise we take and how we bring our children up.'[20]

But that does not appear to be how the food industry sees it. Initiative after initiative shows that the food industry is taking obesity extremely seriously. So much so, it has willingly adopted the role of scapegoat, and is suffering because of it. Food companies are clearly worried that obesity in their customers today could come back to bite them financially tomorrow, just as smoking-related illness has hit tobacco companies. In the United States, McDonald's (in 2002) and Kraft (in 2003) have been sued (unsuccessfully) for selling unhealthy foods, with particular reference in both cases to the vulnerability of children. In a sign of things to come, John Banzhaf, the American 'public interest lawyer', is turning his attention from tobacco to food companies.

There is little doubt that the UK media see 'junk food' or 'fast food' as the cause of the obesity 'crisis'. The fact that these two terms have become interchangeable is interesting in itself. Whereas convenience used to be a good thing, it is now seen as bad: anything that is convenient must also be unhealthy 'junk'. The following headlines give a flavour of the media's general attitude: 'Blame the Junk Food';[21] 'Junk Culture "Is Poisoning Our Children" ';[22] 'Blame Junk Food';[23] 'Junk Food Diet is Blamed for Children's Learning Difficulties';[24] 'Junk Food Makes Teens Depressed';[25] 'Revealed: How Food Giants Use "Dirty Tricks" to Target Children'.[26]

The headlines contributed to the overall assumption that the food industry was to blame for increases in obesity levels. In July 2006, Prime Minister Tony Blair said that if food companies didn't do anything about obesity and food quality, the government would need to step in to make them do it.

Didn't do anything? The food industry has done an enormous amount in recent years to engage in this debate and be seen to do its bit:

- *Food companies have changed their products, by reformulating them to contain less salt, less sugar and less fat, to increase choice and to cut out larger portion sizes.* McDonald's has famously stopped 'supersizing' meals and started offering salads and bagels. On salt content, UK branches of McDonald's have reduced the salt content in chips, Burger King has done the same and Heinz has reduced 11 per cent of the salt in its tomato soup. In November 2006, Unilever announced that it had eliminated 2000 tonnes of salt from its soups – advertised as being the equivalent to 57 Olympic-sized swimming pools.

- *Food companies have changed their labels, to show consumers what is contained in the product in terms of fat, salt, sugar and so on.* There are now two rival labelling schemes, which in itself has been a matter of some controversy. One displays a traffic light colour code to indicate high, medium and low levels of fat, sugar and salt. One uses a Guideline Daily Amount (GDA) system, which labels foods according to a percentage of an individual's recommended daily allowance. Whichever scheme you prefer, it is clear that British food has never been so clearly labelled.

- *Food companies have changed their advertising, to stress to consumers that they should 'enjoy responsibly' or 'be treatwise' and to stop advertising to children.* In January 2005, Kraft announced that it would not directly market many of its foods to children. The *Financial Times* described it as 'one of the industry's biggest concessions yet to anti-obesity campaigners'.[27] In 2006, Kellogg's and Nestlé announced their intention to ban children from their websites to shield them from promotions for sweet, salty and fatty foods.

- *Food companies have changed their marketing initiatives, to include initiatives aimed at helping combat obesity.* In 2004, PepsiCo spent £3 million giving away 5 million pedometers. McDonald's has conducted a similar scheme with 'Happy Meals'. Cadbury-Schweppes misjudged this one, getting into reputational hot water with a scheme in which consumers could save up chocolate wrappers and send off for sporting equipment.

But these initiatives have not had the desired effect. Despite all of the above (and much, much more from other food companies), the British government has recently introduced a ban on 'junk' food advertisements. In November 2006, communications regulator Ofcom announced that 'junk' food advertisements during television programmes that targeted under-16-year-olds would be banned in stages. The ban was imposed despite the fact that Markos Kyprianou, the European Health and Consumer Affairs Commissioner, had indicated that he thought industry self-regulation was working: 'The approach we have chosen is to try first the self-regulatory approach so we are challenging the industry to come out with specific commitments. I think it's working.'[28]

The food industry was not impressed by the UK ban. But it only has itself to blame. The industry allowed the issue of obesity to be discussed in a one-dimensional way. And, with all its social responsibility initiatives, the food industry succeeded only in reinforcing perceptions that it was entirely responsible for the obesity epidemic.

So what should or could the industry have been saying and doing? Perhaps the industry could have pointed out the reality of the issue. Cast your mind back to your childhood. What did you eat? Were you on an organic, low-fat, low-sodium, low-sugar diet? I doubt it, as these are fairly new innovations. Did you have more or less access to healthy food then than you do now? Less, I imagine. A quick straw poll of colleagues and acquaintances has revealed that I was not the only one who routinely consumed fish fingers, chips, fatty meat, crisps, fizzy drinks and as many sweets as I could get my hands on. Access to healthy food has increased in recent decades and knowledge of nutrition has also improved. So surely obesity should be declining rather than increasing? If it isn't, what else could have changed? Are people taking less exercise? Are children today less likely to walk or cycle to school than those of a few decades ago? Yes to both questions. It seems that it is trends in 'energy out' rather than 'energy in' that have changed for the worse. The food industry has said this, but not assertively enough. Companies shy away from playing the blame game, even when governments, NGOs and the media are happily pointing the finger at them.

All of the above assumes there is a problem with obesity in the first place. In November 2006, the *Sunday Telegraph* published an article by two health researchers, which savaged the whole notion of an obesity crisis. The authors point to several pieces of research that question the commonly held beliefs about obesity. They claim that the obesity epidemic is a myth manufactured by public health officials, helped along by academics and special-interest lobby groups. They outline four 'obesity myths': that people, and in particular children, are fat; that being fat means an early death; that obesity stems from food industry marketing; and that people will lengthen their lives only if they lose weight. They warn that the focus on obesity could lead to a generation of children obsessed about their weight – which will lead to an increase in eating disorders – and they conclude: 'The obesity crusade presumes a nursery nation comprised of docile infant-citizens too uncertain of their own values to be left to make their own way in a world in which an evil Ronald McDonald lurks under every archway.'[29]

What is the lesson for CSR from the obesity debate? In my view, food companies could have avoided the entirely unnecessary ban on advertising had they taken a harder line in the debate on obesity rather than pursuing a policy of 'engagement' and misdirected social responsibility. They allowed the CSR initiatives, which looked great on the website and in the social responsibility reports, to reinforce an incorrect public perception that food content is the only cause of obesity. There is only one way the obesity debate is going unless the food industry becomes more assertive and confident about its products, and that is the route that the tobacco companies have been taken down. The industry must start to take on governments and NGOs who use corporate diffidence and compliance to further their own agendas.

In many areas of CSR – not just obesity and climate change – some organizations will find fault with absolutely everything a company does, and some governments will jump on a company's benevolence or willingness to engage as a sign of weakness that can be further exploited. This criticism of companies investing in communities, for example, comes from a Corporate Watch report:

> Community investment covers a whole range of initiatives including: running health programmes, sponsoring schools, playgrounds or community centres, employee volunteering schemes, or signing a memorandum of understanding with communities affected by a company's impacts. However, this creates concerns around companies taking on public functions, and public spaces becoming private.[30]

So, even good initiatives are bad initiatives if companies are involved! I suspect that if ExxonMobil found a miraculous way of reversing global warming, certain organizations would accuse it of 'greenwash' and profiteering.

Again, it appears that, in the hostile external climate, you're damned if you do and damned if you don't. Other authors have put this more eloquently: 'Even those following the highest standards of corporate governance and responsibility have no guarantee of fair treatment, let alone approval. But this, we argue, is no reason not to engage with, and respond accountably to, the widening range of social, environmental and economic issues that society expects business to address.'[31] Whilst I agree with this sentiment, and whilst I would encourage companies not to stop the good work they do just because they are not appreciated, I do wish we could move away from the language of 'engaging with' and 'responding to'. Companies must *lead* this CSR debate. In the absence of corporate leadership, others are leading the debate into increasingly hostile territory.

CSR reports are a waste of time and trees

If environmental responsibility is about preventing the waste of precious natural resources on flippant and unnecessary modern innovations, corporate responsibility reports must be about the most environmentally irresponsible products in the world.

Ben and Jerry's was the first company to publish a CSR report in 1989, but the reports remained fairly marginal until Shell published one in 1998. Nowadays, 90 of the top 100 European companies publish CSR reports, whilst 59 of the US top 100 companies do the same. According to some estimates, by 2005 approximately 1,800 companies were producing CSR reports.[32]

Let's say each of these 1,800 CSR reports has a print run of 1,000 (a conservative estimate as most of the reports are distributed in multiple markets). That would mean the total number of hard-copy reports put into circulation is 1,800,000. And if each report is 200 pages long, that would be 360 million pages. That is a lot of trees... although they are all printed on recycled paper, of course.

And who is reading them? Who on the corporate stakeholder list has got the time, the inclination and the patience to read your corporate responsibility report? Consumers aren't even sent them. Governments and regulators cannot possibly have time to read them. The odd journalist might flick through one, but probably with a sceptical eye. That leaves NGOs, competitors and the CSR industry as the most likely audience for CSR reports. And they are reading the reports with a big red pen at the ready looking for examples of 'greenwash' and 'corporate gloss'. The document might be reporting some good initiatives but, as a communications tool, it is utterly pointless.

But not only are they read primarily by people who are sceptics, there is something wrong with the content of these reports too.

Let's take a fictional example: a chocolate company called PureChoc. PureChoc publishes an annual CSR report, which includes updates on efforts it is making to address concerns about the livelihoods of cocoa farmers around the world. It has a case study of a farmer who is worried about his children's future and the sustainability of cocoa farming in his country. The farmer believes that PureChoc is 'on the right tracks' but there is 'still some way to go'. An 'opinion former', such as an academic at the local university, gives their view on PureChoc's operations in that country. The CSR brochure also includes a report card, showing that the company is making good progress against its self-imposed targets for various things, including local resourcing and emissions reduction. PureChoc has now extended this to reporting against standards that others have set, and this is now being audited by a third party. Also included in the report are stories about local community initiatives that PureChoc is running in Ghana, Nigeria and Brazil to support health and education in cocoa farming communities. Some of them are brand-led, such as the Melters Chocolate Bike Club, which provides branded bicycles for children to get to school from their farms, whilst others are more corporate initiatives such as sponsorship (unbranded) of a new community hospital.

All of this sounds great, and PureChoc is understandably proud of its efforts. But there are two connected problems with this approach. First, and in line with the earlier part of this chapter, the premise of the CSR report is entirely negative. The action may be positive and highly commendable, but it is based on a negative assumption: 'You're all concerned about how we treat cocoa farmers in the developing world, so this is a report all about our response to those concerns.' It is essentially saying: 'You think we're irresponsible; we want to prove that we're not.'

Second, there is only a fleeting mention in the PureChoc report of the growth the company has experienced in the past few years, the profit it is generating, the jobs it has created, the customers it is attracting and the economic development it has encouraged in developing countries. This is deemed 'too corporate' and is left for other documents.

The only redeeming feature about CSR reports is that they can be good for internal purposes. Everyone wants to work for a good company. But there must be ways of showing current and potential employees that their employer is good without persisting with these dreary, defensive, misguided and largely unread social responsibility reports.

The concept of corporate citizenship is more helpful than that of CSR

Corporate social responsibility is an odd phrase, which, as mentioned in Chapter 1, seems to mean different things to different people. In my view, there is something slightly sinister and negative about it. If one of your friends or family members suddenly started being extra nice and going out of their way to do things for you, you would probably start to think to yourself: 'Hang on a minute, what's all this about? What is he/she being so nice for?' If they then explained to you that their good deeds and words were part of an initiative to be socially responsible, you would start to think that they had *really* done something bad.

It is the same with CSR. The phrase comes from a shared assumption that there is something potentially or actually wrong with companies and their contribution to society. It suggests that corporate entities are not intrinsically socially responsible, requiring instead a programme of activities and promises to make them palatable to the world. By buying in to this concept, companies are therefore tacitly accepting the external mindset that they need to make up somehow for the fact that, without CSR, they are bad news. No wonder people think that companies are unethical or irresponsible: even the language we use encourages them to enter a mindset where ethics and responsibility are up for debate. Even the many positive things companies do are presented in a climate of negativity.

The language of 'corporate citizenship' is much more helpful. It is far more positive and describes more accurately the desired positioning of companies in wider society. Good companies should behave like good citizens. They should obey the law wherever they find themselves in the world. They should be respectful and helpful neighbours. They should be sensitive to other people's feelings and needs. They should think about wider society's needs as well as their own. They should respect the opinions of others. They should feel free to speak out when they have an opinion.

The company as a good corporate citizen is also a far more accessible concept to employees, customers and others. Imagine you are the average employee or average consumer. Which of the following two sentences sounds more convincing? 1) As part of our commitment to corporate social responsibility, we have initiated a new energy efficiency programme. Or 2) We as a company want to be a good citizen and a good neighbour, so we have started a new programme to become more energy efficient.

Chapter 3 urged companies to put reputation genuinely at the heart of business. Changing the language of corporate social responsibility to that of corporate citizenship and neighbourliness would be a step along the way to making reputation more accessible.

Performance matters more

I recently had an awful customer services experience with UK satellite TV provider Sky (British Sky Broadcasting). I had to endure weeks and weeks of absolute incompetence from its call centres, various failed attempts to install a satellite dish because it had sent the wrong teams and no recognition that I might have a job that means I can't sit at home every day waiting for them to arrive. It was by far the worst customer experience I have ever had.

I recently read that Sky had committed to going carbon neutral and had joined the Climate Group. CSR professionals at CSR conferences might be impressed with this, but as a consumer, I couldn't care less. To me, they have been irresponsible. Sky has badly let me down and has failed in its first obligation: customer satisfaction.

The point is that good CSR does not compensate for poor customer service or poor performance. It seems odd, for example, that Marconi is listed as a socially responsible company in the FTSE 4 Good index (an ethical stock index). Presumably it meets all the criteria for being an 'ethical' or 'responsible' company. But Marconi has been in perpetual crisis for years and is delivering atrocious commercial performance. What is so socially responsible about corporate failure? One commentator puts this well when he says: 'Most interpretations of "corporate social responsibility" or "corporate citizenship" strike me as a bit fluffy, overemphasizing the "doing good" part of the "doing well and doing good" total formula. Few integrate the whole picture or see the interdependencies.'[33]

Thankfully, it seems that the general public understands that social responsibility starts at home and that it cannot be divorced from performance. A survey in the United States in 2006 found that, when asked to name a socially responsible company, consumers named Wal-Mart as the most responsible company, with McDonald's and Microsoft in second and third place.[34] That seems odd because, according to some journalists and campaigners, these are precisely the brands we are all supposed to hate. But perhaps what the survey respondents are actually saying is that these companies are companies that they like. They are companies that *deliver*. They promise something and, by and large, they deliver it.

In a similar vein, another poll found that 83 per cent of British people say that a company's social responsibility is an important consideration when they are purchasing a product or service. But in the same survey only around a third could name a company that had taken an ethical stance or give an example of corporate support for the community.[35]

This disconnect between what consumers want and what social responsibility campaigners want them to want is a challenge for companies. Dan Rees, Director of the Ethical Trading Initiative, says that 'despite the growing pressures on UK retailers to address consumers' ethical concerns, they face much greater pressure to deliver the cheapest products in the shortest possible time'.[36] This is absolutely right, but it doesn't absolve companies from being good corporate citizens.

The best way to solve this conundrum is to think as a corporate citizen. Every citizen looks out for themselves first and wants to get on and succeed, and the best way to do this is to be good at what you do and to meet people's expectations of you. If you do this in a way that shows people that you are a nice person too, then you are building an even stronger reputation for yourself.

Again, there are parallels in how we feel about each other on a personal basis. Nobody likes arrogant social climbers who display their wealth and build electric fences around their houses, however much we might suspect this person is contributing to the economy. But we also do not necessarily warm to people who are well-meaning and 'kind' but never make anything of themselves or make any contribution to society. We tend to like people who try to do the best for themselves and their families, and we enjoy their success as long as we feel that they are decent neighbours and citizens. Being a good company, therefore, involves being successful and meeting consumer needs whilst going about your business as a good corporate citizen.

For example, Cadbury Schweppes is generally an admired company. But it is an incredibly successful and profitable company, which makes its money primarily from sugary sweets and drinks. Furthermore, it went through a major product contamination scare and recall in the United Kingdom in the summer of 2006. Its reputation did not suffer as badly as some commentators had predicted. Why? Because it is a loved and trusted brand that has provided quality products for years, and has a history of corporate citizenship that dates back to the Cadbury brothers' era. Does that mean that consumers could give an example of a Cadbury Schweppes CSR initiative? Probably not. But they know that the company has delivered in the past, and will deliver again in the future.

CSR promises and initiatives do not significantly affect how people think about a company and whether or not they buy its products and services. Good performance adds to the credit in the reputation bank far more than good CSR. But the better way to see this is to accept that 'doing good' and 'doing well' are indivisible in the corporate mindset.

Although this is a chapter on CSR, and although the term features in the title of this book, I would love to see the end of CSR as a term. This is because the CSR agenda is not a debate about how companies can use their powers, their expertise and their money to ensure capitalism and globalization benefit the many not the few. It is a debate about how the world works, with a vociferous lobby saying that whatever companies do is for the detriment of the world.

The baby should not be thrown out with the bath water though. Companies must still recognize the value of being good businesses and good corporate citizens. But they can and should do this on their own terms, as a confident statement of their worth rather than as an apology. Are there any senior corporate executives out there willing to lead the debate into more positive territory?

To conclude this chapter, my top 10 recommendations on corporate citizenship are listed in the box overleaf.

Top 10 recommendations on corporate citizenship

1. *Move away from the language of CSR* It is premised on a negative, and only reinforces the incorrect external assumptions about what businesses can offer.

2. *Always strive to be a good business* Good businesses are successful businesses. Shareholders must be convinced that money spent on being a good business is money well spent.

3. *Change the premise of the responsibility debate* The starting point for these conversations should not be: 'What can we do to make business more palatable?' but: 'What can we do to be a force for good and show that we are a force for good?'

4. *Focus on performance* Real consumers still judge companies primarily on the customer experience and their ability to deliver. Good initiatives will get lost if the company is not performing.

5. *Merge 'doing well' and 'doing good'* Success is to be celebrated, as it shows that you are perceived to be a good company. Success delivers the resources to make even more of a positive contribution.

6. *Reclaim the language of 'corporate citizenship'* This terminology is far more accessible and better describes a company's role in society.

7. *Resist attempts to turn good business into regulation* A box-ticking approach to being a good business stifles initiative, is not sustainable and is counterproductive.

8. *Scrap the CSR reports* Think of more creative and less wasteful ways to explain to your audiences how you are being a good business.

9. *Always think of the real audience* Never design initiatives to please those who oppose you.

10. *Spread 'good business' through the organization* Use the language and mindset changes above to help ensure that good business and corporate citizenship are understood and 'experienced' through the organization.

Notes

1. Corporate Watch (2006) *What's Wrong With Corporate Social Responsibility?*. Report available at: http://www.corporatewatch.org/?lid=2670. Accessed on: 13 June 2007.

2. Friedman, M (13 September 1970) 'The Social Responsibility of Business is to Increase its Profits' *New York Times Magazine.*

3. European Commission (2001) *Promoting a European Framework for Corporate Social Responsibility*, Green Paper, European Commission.

4. This is a long-running initiative in which Tesco customers can collect vouchers that can then be turned into computer equipment for local schools.

5. This campaign is run alongside charities and provides funds for people in developing countries to have cataract surgery.

6. Chapter 5 discussed concerns about signing up to standards and codes, so this chapter will not repeat that argument.

7. *The Guardian* (7 May 2003) 'Morals Maze', *Society Supplement.*

8. Corporate Watch – see Note 1.

9. Craig Bennett, quoted in *The Guardian* (6 November 2006) 'Promises of Green Energy Fuel Expectations'.

10. European Commission (2002) *Corporate Social Responsibility: A Business Contribution to Sustainable Development*, Employment and Social Affairs Directorate, European Commission.

11. Ibid., p 10.

12. Hilton, S and Gibbons, G (2002) *Good Business*, Texere, London, p 117.

13. An encouraging sign from the Commission more recently: Industry Commissioner Gunter Verheugen told the *Financial Times* that: 'Originally the Commission's plans looked very different. The Department responsible wanted to publish naming-and-shaming lists [of companies] and to create a monitoring system for the implementation of the CSR principles. I had to halt this enthusiasm for regulations.' *Financial Times* (13 March 2006) 'Brussels to Side with Business on CSR'.

14. SustainAbility (2004) *The Changing Landscape of Liability: A Director's Guide to Trends in Corporate Environmental, Social and Economic Liability*, co-produced by Swiss Re, Insight Investment and Foley Hoag LLP, p 13. Available at: http://www.sustainability.com/insight/liability-article.asp?id=180. Accessed on: 13 June 2007.

15. *The Economist* (25 February 2006) 'Staying Pure – Face Value', p 78.

16. *The Sunday Times* (4 March 2007) 'Starbucks Serves up a Storm in a Coffee Cup'.

17. *Seattle Post-Intelligencer* (15 December 2006), 'Does Starbucks Really Care?'
18. *The Seattle Times* (6 March 2007) 'Steaming Ethiopian Coffee Feud Hits at Image Starbucks Cultivates'.
19. *Houston Chronicle* (10 March 2007) 'Starbucks vs Ethiopia'.
20. *The Daily Mail* (25 August 2006) '13m Obese by 2010'.
21. *The Daily Mail* (14 March 2007).
22. *The Daily Telegraph* (12 September 2006).
23. *The Daily Telegraph* (4 August 2006).
24. *The Times* (4 February 2006).
25. *The Daily Mail* (7 March 2007).
26. *The Independent* (24 November 2006).
27. *Financial Times* (13 January 2005) 'Obesity Fears Prompt Kraft to Stop Targeting Children With Junk Food Ads'.
28. Reuters (15 November 2006) 'EU Resists Calls for Junk Food Ad Regulation'.
29. *The Sunday Telegraph* (26 November 2006) 'Four Big Fat Myths'. Basham and Luik's book *Diet Nation: Exposing the Obesity Crusade* (2006) was published by the Social Affairs Unit.
30. Corporate Watch , p 4 – see Note 1.
31. SustainAbility, p 1 – see Note 14.
32. *Ethical Corporation Magazine* (19 October 2006) 'Corporate Ethical Reporting – Time to Give Up?'
33. Cashman, K (28 November 2006) 'Achieving Corporate Citizenship', *Forbes Magazine.*
34. *Forbes Magazine* (28 November 2006), 'The Best Corporate Citizens'.
35. *The Guardian* (6 November 2006) 'The Rise and Rise of the Ethical Consumer', quoting the Ipsos Mori survey on attitudes to business behaviour (see http://www.ibe.org.uk/Briefing_4_Surveys07.pdf).
36. *The Guardian* (6 November 2006), 'Ethical Traders Work Overtime to Help: Who Benefits When Big Companies Get Together and Demand that their Suppliers Adhere to a Code of Practice?'.

7 Turning the corner – the corporation on the couch

All companies have personalities. A recurring theme of this book is that companies need to be bolder, more assertive and more confident when managing their reputations. But what else might a psychologist make of a company's personality in the current climate of corporate mistrust?

Notes from the psychologist's couch

I now feel that I am getting to the heart of Company X's problems. Fundamentally, X feels that the world is against him. He has consequently developed an inferiority complex, which has led him to take some fairly desperate measures. He is extremely concerned about how he is perceived, and is conscious of his own failings, but his obsessive focus on the negatives is unhealthy.

He has many friends, but seems more concerned about those with whom he doesn't have a good relationship and he speaks almost entirely about the bad things that they say about him. This is perhaps a legacy of his youth, when (according to him) he didn't listen to his friends and acquaintances and was too focused on himself and his own success. He seems to be living in perpetual penance for this, which has resulted in a negative mindset. For example, he has told me that, at social events, rather than socializing with those who like and support him (the vast majority of people as he is a fairly affable and successful fellow), he approaches those who clearly do not like him and spends his entire time trying to persuade them that they should see him differently.

When things go wrong, he seems to manage them reasonably well, but again he falls into the routine of accentuating the negative and eliminating the positive. This seems to reinforce the division between him and those of his acquaintances with whom relations are strained.

He clearly has issues, and might even be going through a full-blown crisis. There are some aspects of his behaviour he needs to be wary of and some he knows he needs to change. But he won't make these changes successfully until he changes his general outlook. I believe that, if I can help him regain his confidence and his self-esteem, he can come through this a much stronger and happier company.

Follow change or make change?

So how can companies start to make the necessary changes to manage risks to their reputation more effectively? First, companies need to adopt a different mindset on change.

Most of the literature on reputation management, crisis management, issues management and CSR talks about change, but talks about it as if it is something that is completely out of companies' control. Change seems to be something that just happens in society, and companies need to make sure they are ready to adapt their strategies to meet the challenges that change brings. This approach assumes that companies follow, rather than lead. Companies certainly need to be aware of societal trends, and need to be conscious that they are now, as described in Chapter 2, perpetually under fire. But there is nothing to stop companies actually leading change themselves. Put simply, I would like to see more companies rejecting the mindset of 'The world is changing, we need to be prepared' and adopting a mindset of 'The world is changing, and we can shape the change.'

So, what does the future hold? Could obesity take over from tobacco as a health issue with lawsuits? Perhaps, if the climate of corporate responsibility over individual responsibility further develops. Could corporate reporting on social responsibility become mandatory? Perhaps, if the negative premise of 'social responsibility' remains unchallenged. Could every profit announcement by a global business be a risk to reputation? Perhaps, if the anti-profit and anti-corporate external mindset takes hold.

With the future looking like this, and much more besides, companies need to stop engaging with other people's agendas and start regaining control of the agenda. They need to stop reacting, and start leading.

Leading change in reputation management

This book has encouraged companies to regain the initiative on reputation management. It has argued that, to lead this change, companies need to:

- truly understand the meaning and value of reputation and ensure it permeates in a positive way through the entire company (not just the boardroom and the communications department);
- understand why there is increasing hostility to companies and assess the new risks associated with the 'corporation under fire', but never allow this negativity to take hold;
- change the corporate mindset – build confidence within the company that it is a force for good in the world and celebrate success and achievements;
- change how stakeholders are viewed, prioritized and treated;
- be prepared to defend their reputation against acute risks (crises), but ensure they are crisis-ready for 2010, not 1990;
- adopt a proactive and confident approach to managing the chronic risks to reputation (issues), controlling the agenda and being assertive where necessary;
- rethink the concept and practice of corporate social responsibility, moving away from its negative premise to a more positive emphasis on being a good business and a good corporate citizen.

Companies have been the driving force behind progress and development in the world for hundreds of years. But, thanks to the many changes that have happened in the world in recent years, they have lost their leadership role and are often viewed with suspicion and mistrust. This must be changed. Companies can and should take positive steps to stand up for themselves, manage these external changes and lead change in the future. Any leadership expert will tell you that leadership is not just about navigating the choppy waters and coming through with as few bruises as possible, it is about asserting control over the present and building consensus and support around a positive vision of the future.

Corporate reputation management needs this sort of leadership and change.

Further reading and information

Books

Alsop, J (2006) *The 18 Immutable Laws of Corporate Reputation: Creating, Protecting and Repairing Your Most Valuable Asset*, Kogan Page, London.

Balmer, JMT and Greyser, SA (2003) *Revealing the Corporation: Perspectives on Identity, Image, Reputation and Corporate Branding*, Routledge, London.

Basham, P and Luik, J (2006) *Diet Nation: Exposing the Obesity Crusade*, Social Affairs Unit, London.

Dezenhall, E and Weber, J (2007) *Damage Control: Why Everything You Know about Crisis Management Is Wrong*, Portfolio, New York.

Doorley, J and Garcia, HF (2005) *Reputation Management: The Key to Successful Corporate and Organizational Communication*, Routledge, London.

Elliot, D (2006) *Key Readings in Crisis Management: Systems and Structures for Prevention and Recovery*, Routledge, London.

Fombrun, C (1995) *Reputation: Realizing Value from the Corporate Image*, Harvard Business School Press, Boston, MA.

Fombrun, C and Van Reil, C (2006) *Essentials of Corporate Communication: Implementing Practices for Effective Reputation Management*, Routledge, London.

Genasi, C (2002) *Winning Reputations: How To Be Your Own Spin Doctor*, Palgrave Macmillan, Basingstoke.

Hilton, S and Gibbons, G (2002), *Good Business*, Texere, London.

Kotter, JP (1996), *Leading Change*, Harvard Business School Press, Boston, MA.

Larkin, J (2003) *Strategic Reputation Risk Management*, Palgrave Macmillan, Basingstoke.

Mitroff, I (2005) *Why Some Companies Emerge Stronger and Better from a Crisis*, Amacom, New York.

Morley, M (2002) *How to Manage Your Global Reputation*, Palgrave Macmillan, Basingstoke.

Norberg, J (2003) *In Defense of Global Capitalism*, Cato Institute, Washington.

O'Hanlon, W (2005) *Thriving Through Crisis: Turn Tragedy and Trauma Into Growth and Change*, PERIGEE Books, London and New York.

Rayner, J (2001) *Risky Business: Towards Best Practice in Managing Reputation Risk*, Institute of Business Ethics.

Regester, M and Larkin, J (2005) *Risk Issues and Crisis Management*, Kogan Page, London.

Ruff, P and Aziz, K (2004) *Managing Communications in a Crisis*, Gower Publishing Ltd, Aldershot, Hampshire.

Ulmer, R, Sellnow, T and Seeger, MW (2006) *Effective Crisis Communication: Moving from Crisis to Opportunity*, SAGE Publications Ltd, Thousand Oaks, CA.

Journal articles

Green, S, Jones, S and Sidgwick, C (July 2006) The Nestlé issue from an evidence-based midwifery perspective, *British Journal of Midwifery*, **14** (7).

Reports

Baker Panel (2007) *BP U.S. Refineries Independent Safety Review Panel Report*. Available at: http://www.bp.com/.../globalbp/globalbp_uk_english/SP/STAGING/local_assets/assets/pdfs/Baker_panel_report.pdf. Accessed on: 13 June 2007.

Corporate Watch (2006) *What's Wrong With Corporate Social Responsibility?*. Report available at: http://www.corporatewatch. org/?lid=2670. Accessed on: 13 June 2007.

European Commission (2001) *Promoting a European Framework for Corporate Social Responsibility*, Green Paper, European Commission.

European Commission (2002) *Corporate Social Responsibility: A Business Contribution to Sustainable Development*, Employment and Social Affairs Directorate, European Commission.

Hansard Society (2007) *Friend or Foe? Lobbying in British Democracy*. Available at: http://www.hansardsociety.org.uk/node/view/773. Accessed on: 11 June 2007.

Holmes Group (January 2006) *The Holmes Report*, The Holmes Group, London. Holmes Report newsletters are published online at: http://holmesreport.com.

Institute of Business Ethics (February 2007) *Ethics Briefing: Surveys on Business Ethics* (4).

Ipsos Mori (2006) annual survey on attitudes to business behaviour. Available at: http://www.ibe.org.uk/Briefing_4_Surveys07.pdf.

7 July Review Committee (June 2006) *Report of the 7 July Review Committee*. Available at: http://www.iwar.org.uk/homesec/resources/7-7/report.pdf. Accessed on: 13 June 2007.

LSE Centre for Civil Society and Centre for the Study of Global Governance (2001) *Global Civil Society 2001*, Oxford University Press, New York.

Stern, N (2007) *The Economics of Climate Change*, Cambridge University Press, Cambridge, UK.

SustainAbility (2004) *The Changing Landscape of Liability: A Director's Guide to Trends in Corporate Environmental, Social and Economic Liability*, co-produced by Swiss Re, Insight Investment and Foley Hoag LLP, p 13. Available at: http://www.sustainability.com/insight/research-article.asp?id=46. Accessed on 13 June 2007.

Websites

AccountAbility – http://www.accountability21.net

BBC Editorial Guidelines – http://www.bbc.co.uk/guidelines/editorialguidelines/

Business Continuity Institute – http://www.thebci.org

Business for Social Responsibility – http://www.bsr.org

Business in the Community – http://www.bitc.org.uk

Chartered Institute of Public Relations (CIPR) – http://www.ipr. org.uk/

CSR Europe – http://www.csreurope.org/www.csreurope.com

CSR Newswire – http://www.csrwire.com

Dow Jones Sustainability Group Index – http://www.sustainability-index.com

Ethical Corporation Magazine – http://www.ethicalcorp.com/

European Sustainability and Responsible Investment Forum – http://www.eurosif.info/

Financial Services Authority – http://www.fsa.gov.uk

Fortune Global 500 list – http://money.cnn.com/magazines/ fortune/global500/2006/

Fortune: America's Most Admired Companies – http://money.cnn. com/magazines/fortune/mostadmired/2007/index.htmlhttp: //money.cnn.com/magazines/fortune/mostadmired

FTSE 4 Good index – http://www.ftse4good.com

GoodCorporation – http://www. goodcorporation.com

Institute of Business Ethics – http://www.ibe.org.uk

International Association of Business Communicators – http://www. iabc.com

International Chamber of Commerce – http://www.iccwbo.org

League of American Communications Professionals – http://www. lacp.com

London School of Economics Centre for the Study of Global Governance – http://www.lse.ac.uk/Depts/global/

NGO Watch – http://www.ngowatch.org

PRWeek – http://www.prweek.com;, http://www.prweek.co.uk

Public Relations Society of America – http://www.prsa.org

Reputation Institute – http://www.reputationinstitute.com

Social Investment Forum – http://www.socialinvest.org

UK government gateway to Corporate Social Responsibility – http:// www.csr.gov.uk

What is a Non-Governmental Organization? (City University, London) – http://www.staff.city.ac.uk/p.willetts/CS-NTWKS/ NGO-ART.HTM

World Business Council for Sustainable Development – http://www. wbcsd.ch

Index